CW00839942

BLOODY PRESTON

Bloody Preston

THE BATTLE OF
PRESTON, 1648

Stephen Bull and Mike Seed

Carnegie Publishing Ltd, 1998

© Stephen Bull and Mike Seed, 1998

First published in 1998 by
Carnegie Publishing Ltd,
Carnegie House
Chatsworth Road
Lancaster
LA1 4SL

All rights reserved
Unauthorised duplication
contravenes existing laws

ISBN 1-85936-041-6

Typeset by Carnegie Publishing, Carnegie House,
Chatsworth Road, Lancaster
Printed and bound by Bookcraft (Bath) Ltd

Contents

Acknowledgements

UMEROUS libraries, archives, museums and individuals have provided help in the writing of this book. Space precludes the detailed acknowledgement of all, yet it would be churlish to ignore the very significant contributions of the following: the British Library, Lancashire County Library, Staffordshire County Library, York Minster Library, Lancashire Record Office and Staffordshire Records Office have provided the vast majority of the printed books, pamphlets, original manuscripts and maps. Museums have also been most helpful, regarding both information and access to artefacts. Most importantly these have included Lancashire County Museums, York Castle Museum, the Harris Museum, Preston, and Warrington Museum.

Stuart Reid, an acknowledged expert on the Scottish armies of the seventeenth and eighteenth centuries, has been unstinting in his assistance in an otherwise difficult and obscure area. Keith Matthews at York Castle Museum has helped with access to the Timperly collection of arms and armour. Thom Richardson and Philip Lankester of the Royal Armouries, John Tincey, Gill Chitty, Lancashire County Archaeologist, and Dr Charles Esdaile of Liverpool University have also made valuable comment. David Ryan, who seems to know every Civil War academic, enthusiast and re-enactor, has more than once provided us with the right contacts. One could not end such a list without at least mentioning Professor Austin Woolrych, formerly Pro-Vice Chancellor of Lancaster University, whose pioneering work, published in 1961, demonstrated not only the importance of the battle of Preston but what might be possible given the luxury of a broader canvas. The authors naturally beg their respective families' forgiveness for the many hours spent on this apparently inexhaustible subject, and accept responsibility for any imperfection in the resultant daub, but crave the reader's indulgence on the grounds that this is the first full length work on the battle and that such flaws may be amended by future hands.

S. Bull, M. Seed, Preston

King Charles I on horseback, as depicted on a coin from the
Royalist mint at Oxford during the First Civil War.

Introduction

T IS PARADOXICAL THAT THE MOST IMPORTANT BATTLE of the English Civil Wars should be one of the least well known, yet 'Bloudy Preston' (as it was tagged in at least one contemporary account) is at once both critical for the course of British history, and moderately obscure. Those damp August days three hundred and fifty years ago brought together in one of the largest battles of the period the best that Parliament could field, against a massive Scottish army, and a diminutive yet loyal veteran force of English Northern Royalists. However, this was not only the culmination and climax of a significant campaign, it was a dramatic escalation of the stakes over which Charles I and his Parliament had already fought an expensive and sanguinary four-year conflict.

The 'Great' or First Civil War of 1642 to 1646 had been hard fought, and sometimes bitter, but Edgehill, Marston Moor, Naseby and all the lesser engagements and sieges of that period, were fought for relatively limited objectives. War had started over control of the militia, but control of military force was surely only a part of the equation. Had Parliament been able to part the King from his 'evil' counsellors, remove foreign and papist influences, and limit his apparent willingness to make fast and loose with taxes and monopolies, the members would have been more than satisfied. So it was that, having thoroughly beaten the Royalist forces and captured 'the person' of his Majesty, the King remained king, and was still allowed to be in a position to negotiate. On offer in the 'Heads of the Proposals' at the end of the First Civil War was a settlement which, although it left the army in the control of Parliament, it also included a fair measure of religious toleration and the promise of parliaments of limited duration. There was no question but that the monarchy would remain: Charles would be somewhat chastened and circumscribed, but the aims of the main body of the 'rebels' in 1646 amounted to modification, and a change in the balance of power moderated by tradition, rather than 'revolution'.

The Second Civil War, ultimately decided on the fields around Preston with musket, sword and pike, changed all this. It ended the possibility of a lenient negotiated peace and set in train the events which would lead to the scaffold. Rather than be offered a compromise, the king would face an ultimatum; refusal to bow to it quickly enough would leave him facing a charge. He was to be held responsible for having 'levied and maintained a cruel war', of infinite mischief, which had led to economic ruin and literally to 'thousands of people murdered'. With Preston, English history moved into new and uncharted waters; kings had been deposed, killed on the battlefield, or murdered, but they simply did not stand public trial. In the medieval paradigm, another king, another dynasty, filled the vacuum instantly; or claimed that their kingship predated that of the pretender not yet cold. The Second Civil War opened an apparently unique path to Commonwealth and Republic.

It was also true that 1648 marked a broadening out of the English Civil Wars into something more akin to a struggle for supremacy within the British Isles. England had fought Scotland in 1639 and 1640, and had faced rebellion in Ireland in 1641 and 1642. The Great Civil War, then, marked a nadir in England's fortunes; fighting not only herself but Scottish, Welsh, and Irish forces allied to one side or the other. Seen in this light Preston was the beginning of England's revival, the first clear-cut and catastrophic defeat of a Scottish invasion in memory.

After this the battle lines in the 'divided kingdoms' of Britain would be more apparent, and the outcomes more evidently successful for the country which was destined to become the senior partner in the 'United Kingdom'. Cromwell's tragic Irish campaigns, the war in Scotland in 1650 and the final defeat of another northern invasion at Worcester the following year, all helped to make clear the direction in which the tide was creeping. The monarchy would ultimately be restored but the fate of the ruling house had become inextricably bound up in the 'British' struggle. The Stuart dynasty had certainly been Scottish, in the person of James I of England, and VI of Scotland, and had Scottish and Irish leanings in the later Stuarts. Yet by the eighteenth century they were dispossessed 'Pretenders' of ill-defined European extraction, no more identifiable with any of their peoples than the representatives of the Houses of Orange and Hanover which would supplant them.

Arguably the Second Civil War was a vital turning point, and Preston was indubitably its deciding battle. Yet the outcomes were by no means certain; the decisions balanced on a knife edge, and at more than one point seemed very likely to come down in favour of Charles I and his Scottish allies. Only too understandably did the leading players look to God and Providence for the outcome, for there was no other way by which it could be foretold. Though the politics of the period and the biographies of the most important characters have been well rehearsed, the battle and the mechanics of those few vital days have hitherto received less than their deserved attention. Naseby and Marston

Oliver Cromwell as Lord Protector: a portrait bust in the
classical style from a coin of the 1650s.

Moor have to date more than one eponymous full-length study; each also has
a strong body of opinion, albeit not always heard, in favour of the retention
of the battlefield as a site of historic interest. Preston has the devotion of few
pages of text and scarcely any recognition as a battlefield of note. In the view
of the 'Establishment' and the bureaucrats charged with the listing of such
things the most significant British battle of the seventeenth century does not
even exist.

To be convinced by Preston as an historical event, it needs a character,
a sequence and a description, which would allow the modern viewer to em-
pathise with his forebears who stood in rank against the cut of broadsword
and volley of solid lead shot. What follows is a new attempt to put 'Bloudy
Preston' on our seventeenth-century cognitive map.

An English
Royalist pikeman
reconstructed by
Stuart Peachy. As
seen here, his
equipment is
minimal. He was
probably recruited
in the May of
1648 and equipped
with helmet, pike
and coat, the rest
of his clothing
being his own.

1

Battle in 1648

ATTLES IN THE SECOND CIVIL WAR were no more pleasant than battles in any other era. One should not be fooled by Victorian prints of 'gay' cavaliers or the chivalric conduct of certain generals into thinking that the purpose of armies was other than to overcome the enemy by force; and if necessary to kill his troops more efficiently than his could yours. In some senses Civil War battles were all the more horrifying because much of the slaughter took place at close range; sometimes hand to hand with edged weapons and musket butts. The twentieth century is used to the 'empty battlefield' where troops are spread out and seldom seen. Preston was, by such standards, very crowded; at one moment about 20,000 men occupied the square mile bounded by the Ribble bridge, Ribbleton, the present site of Fulwood Barracks and the north west corner of Moor Park adjoining the A6. Although Preston was then a town of only 2,000 or so there were as many people crowded on to this vital spot as there are today.

The three basic 'arms' of the military in the seventeenth century were the cavalry, infantry and artillery.[1] The infantry were the most numerous and were divided into regiments under colonels. In 1648 regiments varied hugely in strength, from 250 at the weakest through to 1,000 or more for the strongest. Regiments were theoretically composed of ten companies, one for the colonel, one for the lieutenant colonel, one for the major and the rest commanded by captains. This was not always adhered to, particularly in weak regiments. Sometimes the colonel was absent and command of the whole was assumed by the lieutenant colonel, or a company was commanded by a captain-lieutenant.

Each company had its own colours, carried by a junior officer known as an 'ensign' or 'ancient', and there was also a second in command, usually a lieutenant, who would deputise for his captain. It was also usual to have a company clerk, at least one drummer who could also act as a messenger, a couple of sergeants and three corporals. There might also be a number of picked men, lance corporals or file leaders, who would be responsible for their own file of half a dozen, who would eat and sleep as well as march together. The company would seldom operate independently, unless it was part of the 'forlorn hope', but would usually fight as a part of the regiment. Often regiments would be grouped together, forming an *ad hoc* 'brigade'.

The infantry were themselves of two sorts: the musketeers and the pikemen. Occasionally muster roles are encountered with a small 'm' or 'p' beside the men's names denoting the weapon with which they had been issued, for unlike the officers the 'other ranks' were given their weapons and basic equipment, at the expense of parliament or their colonel. Strangely to modern minds, it was the pikeman who was deemed the superior soldier. His weapon was the older and, to mid seventeenth-century way of thought, therefore the more honourable. Pikemen also tended to be better physical specimens for they had to carry a length of ash tipped with steel between 15 and 18 feet in length, standard for the New Model Army being 16 feet. Yet contrary to popular saying pike staffs were not 'plain' in the sense of being the same diameter over their whole length; instead they were carefully shaped so that the thickest part was a little above the butt. This was important since when the pike was levelled in the 'charge' position it brought the centre of gravity as near to the pikeman's

The pike was meant to be a minimum of fifteen feet in length, made of ash and tipped and shod in steel. Left: an early seventeenth-century Dutch illustration of an armoured pikeman.

body as possible, making the weight more bearable. At the business end of the pike was a steel head. Long slender pikeheads are usually construed as 'English' in style, whilst more diamond or lozenge shaped points are thought of as 'Dutch' in influence. 'Cheeks' or 'langets' of metal extended a little way down the shaft of the pike, serving not only to attach the head but making it very difficult for the end to be lopped off.[2]

Traditionally the pikeman had been armoured in a 'corselet' of steel, com-prising a breastplate, back and 'tas-setts' for the thighs, and a helmet or 'pikeman's pott' for the head. Many of these pieces are yet found, bearing the mark for the armourers company of London under Charles I, a crowned 'A', and the initials of the ar-mourer.[3] For a number of reasons it seems unlikely that many of the pikes at Preston would have been ar-moured. In the first place it had proved difficult to get enough armour even in the First Civil War; the royalists in particular were denied ac-cess to the main producing area in London, and were also prevented from obtaining many imports by par-liamentarian control of the sea. In cases where pike armour was short, it became the norm to issue it only to 'file leaders' and 'bringers up' at the rear of each unit. In this way the most vulnerable in the unit were protected whichever way it faced.

From 1645 foot soldiers of the 'New Model' were not issued with armour at all, and for good reason. As a 'national' army the new force was intended to go anywhere and additional encumbrance was a dis-advantage to both strategist and common soldier. Armour was also ex-pensive and most importantly was of dubious utility, as pike armours were

Civil War pikeman's armour, or 'corselet', made in London, c. 1640. By the time of the Battle of Preston few infantry wore any armour, since it was usually incapable of resisting musket balls. (*York Castle Museum*)

Infantry officer's Flemish-style 'Pott' helmet. (*York Castle Museum*)

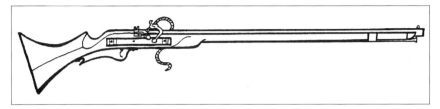

The matchlock musket, the main infantry weapon of the Civil Wars. This example has a 'fish tail'-style butt, popular at the end of the sixteenth and during the early seventeenth centuries.

not proof against the musket. A few commanders continued to believe that pike armour was necessary. Sir James Turner, writing as late as 1670, thought that an army should appear to its enemies as a 'brazen wall' in armour, 'but we shall rarely see a Battalion of pikes in such harness, and no wonder, since the pike itself is not now used as much as it hath been'.[4] In 1610 it had been usual to have roughly equal numbers of pikes and muskets in English regiments, but by 1642 two muskets were allowed for each pike. By the end of the century there might be as many as four firearms for each pike. It is therefore likely that at Preston more than two thirds of the infantry were musket armed.

By 1648 the musket was well on its way to becoming the standard infantry weapon, a process which had been two hundred years in the making.[5] Most muskets were still 'match lock' weapons; by this is meant a gun which was fired by means of a smouldering length of matchcord or 'slow match'. The basic firing procedure was as follows: first a small amount of powder was poured into the 'priming pan' which was then closed; next a full charge of powder and a spherical lead bullet weighing just over an ounce were rammed down the barrel. The smouldering matchcord was now fitted to the 'jaws' of the lock and then the pan was opened and the musket 'presented' ready to fire. Pulling the trigger pushed the cord into the open pan and fire was communicated to the main charge via the 'touch hole' and the musket fired.

Many drill books broke down this procedure into a series of 'postures' or 'motions' each with its own individual command. William Barriffe in his *Militarie Discipline* gave 33, and Gervase Markham in the *Souldier's Exercise* gave 32. If these are run through in a slow and deliberate manner with a reproduction musket it takes over two minutes to fire a shot, but such detailed instruction was intended for training only. As Markham pointed out, 'in the face of the enemie' the commands were reduced to three: 'make ready', 'present', and 'give fire'. A trained man, knowing what to look out for and using maximum economy of movement, could therefore fire every 35 to 45 seconds for a few minutes. Firefights would rarely last much longer and the usual allowance of ammunition was about a dozen rounds.[6]

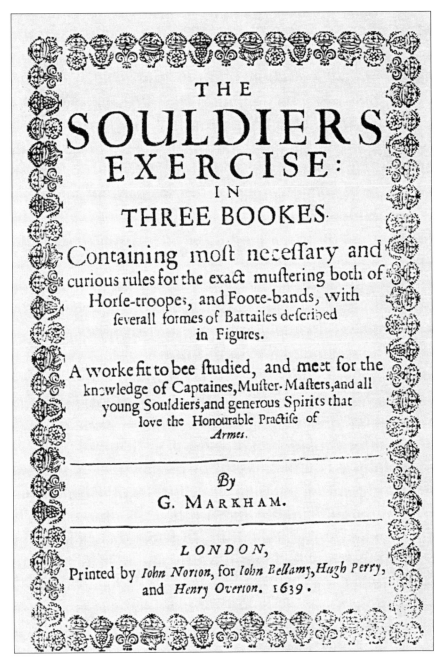

THE
SOULDIERS
EXERCISE:
IN
THREE BOOKES·

Containing moſt neceſſary and
curious rules for the exact muſtering both of
Horſe-troopes, and Foote-bands, with
ſeverall formes of Battailes deſcribed
in Figures.

A worke fit to bee ſtudied, and meet for the
knowledge of Captaines, Muſter-Maſters, and all
young Souldiers, and generous Spirits that
love the Honourable Practiſe of
Armes.

By
G. MARKHAM.

LONDON,
Printed by *Iohn Norton,* for *Iohn Bellamy, Hugh Perry,*
and *Henry Overton.* 1639.

The title page to Gervase Markham's *Soldier's Exercise,* 1639; one of many
drill books available during the civil wars.

Two of the musketeers' 'postures' from De Gheyn's early seventeenth-century Dutch drill book, 'present' and 'give fire'. Notice the 'bandoleers' around the soldiers body with pre-prepared charges. Musket rests, shown here, had generally been discarded some time before 1648.

It is often said that the matchlock was inaccurate, slow and unreliable. Compared to the modern rifle this is true, but in the seventeenth century it was an efficient enough killing machine. Modern tests, at Bisley and elsewhere, have shown that a smooth-bore musket can, more often than not, hit a man-size target at 50 yards and sometimes at 100. In 1648 individual failings were made up for by the fact that the musketeers were deployed in bodies three or six ranks deep, and fired 'en masse' one rank at a time or by salvos. Usually the target was bigger than a single man; a troop of cavalry or a block of pikemen was indeed larger than the proverbial 'barn door'. When a musket ball hit the human frame the effects could be devastating. If not immediately fatal, gangrene, loss of blood and other complications could lead to a lingering death. As John Woodall described in 1617, a gunshot wound was accompanied by 'losse of substance, contusion, fraction of many sinewy fibres, veynes, arteries, membranes and bones, yea often shivered into divers peeces'.

Richard Wiseman, surgeon to Charles II and one time doctor in the royalist army, noticed the strange way that bullets, if they did not exit immediately, could lodge in unexpected places. One soldier, shot in the cheek, had the bullet removed from the back of his neck; another, shot through the sternum, had it taken out at the back! In many cases pieces of clothing driven in by the shot

A musketeer.

caused extra infections. Bullet wounds to the limbs often resulted in amputa-
tion, itself a traumatic and sometimes fatal procedure.

It was true that weather could cause difficulties to musketeers. Strong wind
could blow away loose powder or make accurate fire difficult; rain could make
powder damp or put out the matchcord. But careful soldiers had remedies for
most of the problems. In bad weather both ends of the match would be lit,
which wasted match but made it unlikely that the soldier would be without
fire. Similarly the soldier could use a 'match holder' or little perforated tube

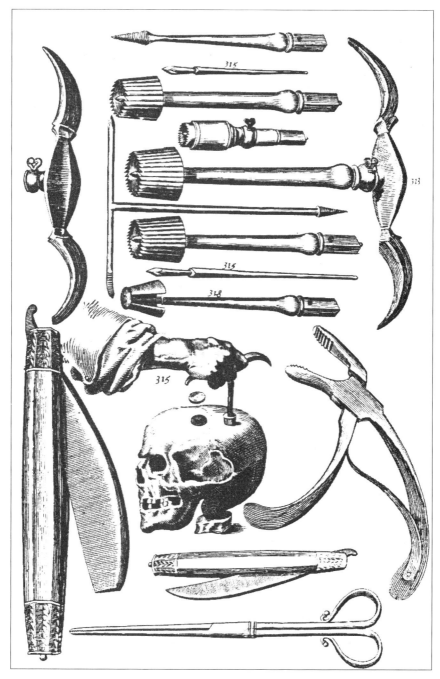

Just a few of the horrors of seventeenth-century surgery, as illustrated in the 1639 edition of John Woodall's medical text book. Shown here are incision razors, forceps for removing bone splinters, and trepanning equipment.

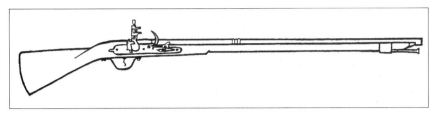

The 'fire lock' musket. Ignited by a flint and steel this weapon was far better suited to skirmishing and to guard duty. Though reasonably common in 1648, flint lock weapons would not entirely supplant match locks until the early-eighteenth century.

which would protect the match from wind and rain. Also one did not always have to pour powder from the wooden charge holders of the 'bandolier', as paper cartridges were not unknown and could be stored in a box or pouch close to the body. Tearing the end of the cartridge and stuffing the paper down the barrel as well as the powder and ball might lead to quick fouling of the barrel, but had advantages where a moving soldier might otherwise let a poorly-fitting shot drop out, or was aiming for maximum speed. A good deal of ramming could be dispensed with by the expedient of banging the musket butt on the ground, a move not calculated to improve accuracy, or the sergeant's temper. Spare match was normally carried in a bundle around the shoulder of the 'file leader' and it has been suggested that the stowed match was the original of the shoulder cord, and later the white chevrons of the corporal.

Tactically pike and musket worked together. The pike was ideal to fend off enemy cavalry since horses were reluctant to run onto a hedge of steel spikes, and also to close with enemy infantry at 'push of pike'. The 'fireman', by contrast, was best fighting at a few yards distant, loading and firing until the enemy wavered and then wading in with 'clubbed musket' and sword. Often one side had broken and run before blows were exchanged.

Other sorts of musket in use in 1648 were the 'doglock', 'English lock', or 'firelock', all of which were early versions of the flintlock, and especially useful for skirmishers or guards.[7] As early as 1642 it was intended to equip a company of each regiment serving in Ireland with 'firelocks'. In the firelock a piece of flint was held in the jaws of the lock; pulling the trigger allowed the flint, under pressure of a spring, to snap against steel and produce a spark. In the 'dog' lock a small safety catch prevented the accidental operation of the lock. The advantages of the firelock were several, the most significant of which was that there was no burning matchcord and thus little possibility of accident, or of betraying a soldier's position at night. Reliability was also improved, as was mobility, and fifty years after the civil war improved 'flintlocks' would be the standard arm. By 1645–46 the English New Model was ordering considerable numbers of firelock weapons, both 'snaphaunce dragoons' and full size muskets – 1,000 muskets were contracted for in April 1645, and a similar order in December. Smaller numbers were also purchased, like the 50 'bought by Lieutenant General Hamond'. The largest order, of 2,200, was received in 1648.[8]

It is therefore reasonable to suppose that the New Model dragoons, and at least ten percent of the infantry, were equipped with firelocks. It has previously been argued that these weapons were concentrated only in the hands of Fairfax's own regiment, but it is far more likely given the numbers that a company in every regiment was so armed, allowing them to provide a 'forlorn hope' of skirmishers, or sentinels, as necessary. Sporting rifles and fowling pieces are also occasionally mentioned in the hands of Civil War snipers and skirmishers, and although none are mentioned in the New Model's papers, it is possible that the royalists or Scots had some. The Scots also had companies of firelocks under Sir Alexander Frazer.

It is interesting to note that there had been changes in infantry tactics since Charles I first went to war with the Scots in 1640. At that time most commanders had still used the 'Dutch' model used by Maurice of Nassau in the Low Countries: infantry regiments had usually fought as one unit with musketeers forming the 'sleeves' or 'wings' and the pikes in the centre. Such formations were eight or ten ranks deep and the musketeers fired by 'introduction' or 'extraduction'. During 'introduction' the rear rank would file to the front of the unit and discharge, followed by each succeeding rank. Once eight or ten ranks had completed their firing the first rank would again be ready to fire. With 'extraduction' the process was similar but in this case the firers retreated to the back of the unit after each discharge. The overall effect was that a unit would keep up a steady fire, whilst either advancing or retreating slowly.

By 1648 most, if not all, armies in Britain were using methods approximating to the 'Swedish' system which had been used by the troops of Gustavus Adolphus in the Thirty Years War. In this deployment it was usual to break down the blocks of musketeers into bodies of 50 or so, with a maximum depth of six. Fire by 'introduction' was still possible but it became normal to fire in salvos, often doubling the files to the front to create a line only three ranks deep. The pikes, now fewer in number, formed solid islands to which the musketeers could retreat in case of danger, or could even be broken down into a single line with which to stiffen the musketeer formations, a deployment apparently known as 'fraised'.[9] The advantages of the Swedish system in terms of flexibility, volume of fire and making a less dense target are all apparent, but it required better training of the men and a skilful body of junior and non-commissioned officers to be carried out successfully. Contrary to popular belief there were therefore significant changes in infantry tactics between 1642 and 1648, with an increasing emphasis on flexibility, firepower and the ability to skirmish. Training and experience would count for even more in the Second Civil War than the first.

Cavalry were very important in 1648, though not as numerous as the infantry, and as in the chivalric hierarchy a horseman was usually considered better than a foot soldier. The basic cavalry unit was the troop, 60 or 80 in strength; New Model regiments had six troops, Scottish regiments three. The commander of a cavalry regiment was its colonel and troops were usually led by officers ranking as captains or higher. The junior officers of the troop were a lieutenant and a 'cornet' who carried the troop 'cornet', the cavalry equivalent of colours. There was also usually a quartermaster and three corporals. Dragoons tended to fight on foot and to follow infantry organisation, usually acted as skirmishers or scouts, and by 1648 were often deployed a couple of troops with each force, rather than as a complete regiment.[10]

The majority of the cavalry were armoured with a helmet, breast and back plate; they normally carried a pair of pistols and a sword. Most of the armour was originally made by the armourers company of London, like the 100 breasts, backs and 'potts' ordered from Anthony Newman, or the 1,000 from Colonel Rowe by the English New Model. Most helmets were of the three barred 'English' or 'Lobster Tailed' type, though older styles may still have been in use with officers who purchased their own, or in the provincial forces. The cavalry breast plate was small, not so much because of the marginal difference in stature between the seventeenth century and the present, but because to withstand a pistol ball armour had to be thick. If armour was thick it was heavy, and therefore in terms of weight it was only practical to cover the most vital organs of chest and stomach.

It is a fallacy that the 'Ironsides' were the only cavalry to wear armour, for royalists also adopted helmets and breast plates whenever they were available. It is also questionable whether heavy leather 'buff' coats were normally worn with armour. The buff coat was an expensive item, and by itself a credible defence against a sword swipe, but it was not an issue item to the English New Model. It is therefore likely to have been limited to those who had been issued with them at an earlier date, or to those, usually officers, who could afford them as a private purchase.

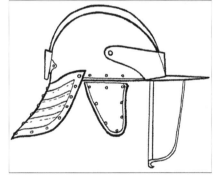

The cavalry trooper's 'pott', or 'lobster pott', helmet. Most English examples of the Civil Wars were fitted with three bars on the face guard; contrary to popular opinion their use was not limited to the troopers of parliament.

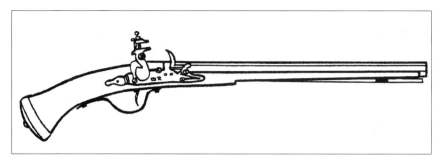

A 'dog lock' cavalry pistol, as used *c*.1648.

By 1648 most cavalry pistols were of 'snaphaunce' or 'dog-lock' types, with a flint sparking against steel; they had largely replaced the more expensive 'wheel locks' which preceded them. A flint striking weapon had the edge, not only in terms of price and ease of production, but because it required no special tool or 'spanner' to cock it. Pistols fired a smaller bullet than the musket and were much less accurate, especially when riding. Few can have been hit with pistol bullets at over 20 yards, and the preferred tactic was to shoot as close as possible. As a last resort a pistol made a passable club, or could even be hurled in the enemy's face as a desperate delaying tactic. C. H. Firth in his remarkable *Cromwell's Army* believed that New Model cavalry carried no carbines; nonetheless over 1,000 of them were purchased in 1646 alone.[11]

The sword was also an important cavalry arm; most were broad bladed with some form of basket hilt. Full-barred baskets were known, as were 'half baskets'. One form of hilt which appears to have been uniquely English was the 'Mortuary' sword, so called because the faces which decorated its hilt were believed by the Victorians to represent the martyred Charles I. Since many similar swords predate 1648 it can be said with confidence that the attribution is incorrect, and that the faces are either simply a decorative style, or represent persons other than the king.

Though the basket and mortuary types can be said to be English, the blades for these swords were often made on the continent, particularly in western Germany; and the same applies to many 'Scottish' basket-hilted broadswords. The only places making blades in England at this time appear to have been Birmingham and Hounslow. Troopers were often issued with cheaper 'munition' swords, whilst officers had the possibility of buying their own higher quality weapons in a variety of styles.[12] A weapon unique to the Scottish cavalry was the lance. Many Scots were conventionally armed with sword and pistols, some of them supplied by the English parliament in 1644–46, but the lance was not only a cheap alternative; it was particularly useful against a scattered or retreating enemy and had a longer 'reach' than the sword.

It is often thought that royalist cavalry, under the influence of Prince Rupert, were dashing and uncontrollable, whilst those of parliament were slower but better disciplined. Although another Victorianism, there is a grain of truth in the argument; most cavalry in 1642, like the infantry, used 'Dutch' tactics. Deep units of horse would ride up to the enemy and, one rank at a time, would trot up, give fire and retire. Prince Rupert was probably one of relatively few young officers who at that date preferred the 'Swedish' methods – riding up in shallow, often three rank lines, and then charging home sword in hand. By 1648 this pattern of attack was probably the norm.

The third arm of the seventeenth-century army was the artillery. It was divided into 'field' and heavier 'siege' pieces. Since a siege battery presented particularly big supply and transport problems it was usually centralised into a 'train' and directed as a unit by

The hilt of a 'mortuary' type sword, *c.*1640.

the army command. Prior to 1642 there had been little uniformity in gun sizes and the pieces were often known by arcane terms such as 'Falcon' or 'Saker', but during the war increased standardisation, particularly on the parliamentarian side, allowed smaller guns to be known by the weight of their shot. Parliamentarian field guns were usually 3-, 6- and 12-pounders and the vast majority of them were supplied by the Browne cartel of the Weald of Kent and Sussex. The Scots had purchased guns from this source, but also made their own, specialising in the lightest most mobile types, including 'leather guns' which were actually small iron pieces bound with leather. Royalist forces, in 1648 as in 1642, were more motley in their equipment. Often they had to rely on out of date relics from castles and forts, or strip guns from ships. Attempts to set up their own foundries and to import foreign guns met with only limited success.[13]

In the battle field artillery was usually set up in small batteries between the leading elements of the foot. There is no evidence that guns were ever used as 'horse' artillery in this period, nonetheless under the right circumstances guns could be quite effective. A six pounder gun could fire almost a mile when elevated, and even when levelled directly at the target could manage 300 yards, or more than double effective musket range. In practice most artillery fire was at 500 yards or less, with solid 'roundshot' used at the more distant targets, and 'cases' of musket balls used for close range work.

Seventeenth-century artillery did not have pinpoint accuracy but a troop of horse, or a regiment of foot, were very big targets and the results could be horrifying. One parliamentarian account of the battle of Newbury noted how 'mens bowels and brains flew in our faces' when standing under fire. A Scottish 'poet' versifying the English infantry under bombardment at Newburn in 1640 described how men were 'dashed' with roundshot, which severed limbs, 'spewed' brains and thundered fit to have riven the 'burnished vaults of heaven'. More detached analysis showed that the roundshot tended to graze or 'bounce' along the ground carving deeply through the ranks; 'case' shot would act like a huge shot gun. Though devastating in the right circumstances, like a protracted set piece battle, artillery was at its least useful in an 'encounter' like Preston, where the Scottish army in particular would be attempting to manoeuvre and then deploy from the columns of march.[14]

The task of the general in the middle seventeenth-century battle was to use and co-ordinate all the elements of his army to defeat his enemy, or to gain strategic or tactical advantage by taking or holding positions. Staff work was generally not good and, though units were usually well structured, higher organisation was often lacking. Messages could be sent by courier, but on the smaller fields of battle it was often as effective for the commander to ride over and give personal direction, perhaps to a general or colonel in charge of a 'brigade' of regiments. Orders were passed down the chain of command, via officers to sergeants and corporals who physically directed the individual soldier. Simple signals, to march or engage, could be given by drum or trumpet, but timing was always difficult as clocks and pocket watches were rare and not usually synchronised.

The best plans were therefore the simplest, and though there was often a conference between brother officers before battle, a tried and tested disposition was often used. If there were changes of plan these were also kept as straightforward as possible, since confusion or loss of cohesion might lead to rout. Usually the army was concentrated and the infantry were drawn out in one or two major lines, the bulk of the cavalry on either flank; the artillery, dragoons and other skirmishers took the front. The bones of such a deployment were used by both sides at Edgehill, Marston Moor, Naseby and several other battles of the first civil war. An added refinement was often the use of a hill or ridge line, which would serve to hide a proportion of the army from the enemy and put an attacker at a disadvantage. This had worked well at Lansdowne, Naseby and Marston Moor, but failed at Edgehill where the royalists descended from their vantage point to attack. At Preston some of the generals would put the theory to good practice, others would ignore it at their peril.

2

The Forces

Parliament: New Model, Northern Association and Militia

RGUABLY THE MOST BATTLE-HARDENED FORCE in the British Isles in 1648 was the New Model Army. The title was due to the 'new modelling' of parliament's armies in the winter of 1644–45 at the height of the First Civil War. What had gone before were not in any sense national armies, but forces created to fulfil an objective, or 'Association' armies raised by specific areas. Although parliament had won a major victory at Marston Moor in July 1644, success was followed by setback when Sir William Waller was defeated at Cropredy Bridge and the army of the Earl of Essex captured at Lostwithiel. It was realised that to complete what had been begun a radical re-organisation was necessary.

The army which was created as a result was centrally administered and would go anywhere at the behest of parliament. More than this the reformation of the army had given the opportunity for lukewarm leadership to be jettisoned. Lords Essex and Manchester may have believed that the king could be brought by campaigning to the negotiating table, but those who succeeded them, Lord Fairfax and his senior commanders, were prepared to prosecute the war to a conclusion in which the Royalist field armies and garrisons were systematically reduced, and the king himself was a prisoner.[1]

The instrument by which this new force would be melded was the 'self denying ordinance' by which members of parliament would agree to relinquish military command to professional soldiers. In practice this would hit hardest at the Lords who had traditionally led the armies, since commoners could make the choice to resign from the house and continue as soldiers. Understandably the Lords did not let the bill pass immediately and instead the Commons had to proceed circuitously, creating a new army and then allowing the old forces to wither through lack of funding. The new army comprising 6,000 horse, 1,000 dragoons and 14,400 foot, rapidly went on to prove its worth, winning a remarkable victory at Naseby in June 1645. In the next year it was the prime instrument with which the war, militarily at least, was brought to a conclusion.

Compared to most forces the New Model had a more uniform appearance. Coat colours were not chosen by individual colonels, but were all red, thigh length and distinguished only by 'facings' where the lining showed and the colour of the tapes which closed them. Breeches were predominantly grey, and like the blue charge 'bandoleers', cartridge boxes, shoes, knapsacks, stockings and shirts were all centrally ordered by the Committee of the Army. The fact that firearms and ammunition were similarly supplied may also point to greater standardisation.

The New Model was not, however, an invincible force, nor was it entirely universal or without flaw. In the first place it did not entirely supplant all existing parliamentary forces; two notable survivors were the Northern Association and the county militias, both of which would have a bearing on the conduct of the Preston campaign. Secondly, although centrally organised and funded, it was not immune to the wants which had bedevilled other armies. Usually pay was well in arrears; it was not that the army went totally unpaid, but that the amount received was never equal to that owed. In many months, instead of getting four weeks pay, the troops would get two or three. Unsurprisingly, therefore, the regiments of the New Model would be loath to disband whilst there were large sums outstanding.

Perhaps most significantly in hindsight, the New Model was not an apolitical body. Ironically, parliament had ensured this when it was constituted; most armies of the period were caricatures of the society from which they were drawn, led by lords, filled with those unable to escape selection from the militia, and leavened with enthusiasts and professionals. The New Model had screened out of it the old pillars of society and concentrated those officers willing to prosecute an aggressive and successful war. At the outset Lords and Commons haggled to fill the officer corps with those whose political opinions were in harmony with their own objectives, and essentially it was an argument that the lower house won. Pay came from parliament, not noblemen, or the counties, and it was to parliament that the new army would make its grievances.[2]

Following the end of the first war, 'Levelling' agitation, and in places outright mutiny, the New Model was re-modelled. Work on the establishment began early in 1647, but a new structure was not finally cleared until February 1648. The total strength was to be 16,000 foot and 6,720 horse, plus 1,000 dragoons. The foot would be in 17 regiments, each with ten companies of 80 men, and there would be 30 'loose' companies for garrison duty. Each regiment would have a colonel as its commanding officer, with a lieutenant colonel and a major to second him. Other companies were led by captains. The junior officers were a lieutenant and 'ensign' per company, the primary duty of the ensign being to carry the company colours.

The horse were also re-modelled into a greater number of slightly smaller units. There would be 14 regiments, each regiment having six troops of 80. The horse regiments were officered in a similar manner to the foot but there was usually no lieutenant colonel, and cavalry standards were smaller and technically known as 'cornets', so the most junior officers of the horse who carried them were also known as cornets, rather than ensigns. Artillery was not comprehensively dealt with in 1647 and the ordnance office which was responsible for supplying the guns would not itself be 'New Modelled' until 1649.[3]

Although Lord General Sir Thomas Fairfax was commander in chief of the New Model, it was Lieutenant General Oliver Cromwell who would command at Preston. Since Cromwell has become one of the giants of English history and folklore it is difficult to be dispassionate about his generalship in 1648, a time before anyone had dreamed that there would be a 'Lord Protector'. It is interesting to note that although Cromwell already had a good deal of experience in military matters, Preston would be the first time he commanded the army in a full scale field battle. Indeed Cromwell may have appeared to his contemporaries as something of a parvenu. Before the war he was a pretty obscure Huntingdon gentleman and Member of Parliament, and without the war he might have remained that way. Even once hostilities had commenced it would take time for him to come to prominence.

At the first major battle, at Edgehill in 1642, Cromwell was only a captain. By 1644 he had risen to lead the cavalry of the Earl of Manchester's Eastern Association army; but Manchester's army was only one of several, and thus it was at Marston Moor, although Cromwell had a significant role, he was only one of several commanders. In what was a huge and often shambolic fight, Cromwell generally seems to have acquitted himself well. He was slightly wounded and, even though his enemies said that he deserted the field for an unconscionable time, was one of those who kept his head when all seemed lost. At Naseby in 1645 his personal contribution was unquestionable, as lieutenant general of the New Model Cavalry much had depended on his ability to deal with Sir Marmaduke Langdale's northern horse. In 1646 and 1647 he had begun to prove his political ability and had become identified with the 'Independents' and the Army, holding the demands of the 'Levellers' at arms length. Whilst Cromwell had demonstrated ability, ambition, confidence and success as a subordinate commander we should not consider the result of Preston in any way a foregone conclusion. Sometimes, indeed, we are not helped to be impartial by Cromwell's own insistence in his letters on the presence of the hand of God, or destiny.

Oliver Cromwell, by Walker, *c*.1649. Few characters of English history have provoked such antithetical reactions, or found such enduring fame. So much so indeed that it is sometimes difficult to believe that before the battle of Preston 'England's Atilla', and future Lord Protector, was just one of several leading parliamentarian generals. The pinnacle of his meteoric rise was reached after 1648, and was built at least in part on his performance in the campaign. (*National Portrait Gallery*)

Four full regiments, and part of a fifth, of New Model horse were at Preston, plus two companies of the dragoons. Cromwell's own regiment was undeniably the best known, but it is not often realised that his personal command had a chequered existence. Cromwell's original 'ironsides' of the First Civil War had been in the pay of the Eastern Association, and by 1644 were at a double regiment strength of 14 troops. With the reorganisation of the army they were split up to make General Fairfax and Colonel Whalley's regiments of horse. Just before Naseby command of Vermuyden's regiment fell vacant and Cromwell was granted this position. Cromwell's new regiment was one of those which led the agitation of 1647, and soon after his Major resigned on the basis that he found the conduct of Cromwell and other senior officers 'very repugnant and destructive'. He was replaced in June 1648 by Major Blackmore, whom Cromwell had recommended as 'a godly man and a good souldier'. Three captains serving in Cromwell's regiment at Preston have been identified: Joseph Wallington, John Spenser and Edward Sexby. The last two named were definitely present, Spenser distinguishing himself during reconnaissance, and the famous leveller Sexby being a messenger to parliament after the battle.

Harrison's regiment of horse had first been led by James Sheffield, one of the many sons of Lord Sheffield. Thomas Harrison, formerly known as the 'praying major' of Fleetwood's regiment, succeeded to the colonelcy during the unrest of 1647. Harrison himself was absent from Preston as a result of a wound received in a skirmish at Appleby on 17 July 1648, but the identity of several of his officers is known. Major William Rainborowe was Harrison's brother-in-law, Captain Henry Cromwell was Oliver's second surviving son. Captain Stephen Winthrop, although born in Suffolk, had spent much of his life in New England where his father was governor of Massachusetts. Other officers thought to be present during the campaign were Captains Whitehead and Peck, and Cornet Day.[4]

Philip Twisleton succeeded as colonel to Rossiter's Lincolnshire regiment of horse in August 1647, a unit in which he had previously been serving as major. With this promotion was created a vacancy which was filled by bringing in James Berry from Fairfax's regiment as the new major. Berry was sent with news of the victory at Preston to parliament and so for the remainder of the campaign his duties were fulfilled by the colourful Hezekiah Haynes. Hezekiah was the son of John Haynes of Copford Hall near Colchester, and John Haynes was to become governor of first Massachusetts and then Connecticut. The names of the other Captains in Twisleton's are known: Henry Markham, Owen Cambridge, John Nelthorp, Bushey and Pearte.

Francis Thornhaugh's regiment of horse was one of the oldest in parliament's armies having been formed in late 1642 and early 1643. Based in Nottinghamshire it fought throughout the First Civil War and Thornhaugh was himself

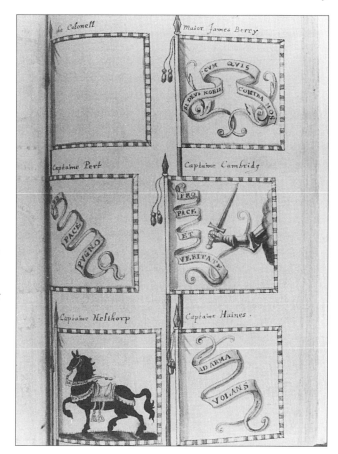

The 'cornets' of Twistleton's New Model regiment of cavalry. Each troop commander had his own cornet, and six troops of 80 men made up the regiment. Illustrated from the Turmile manuscript. (*Dr William's Library*)

wounded twice. Although not initially part of the New Model it was kept in arms after the war. Thornhaugh's major was Thomas Saunders, a man described by Lucy Hutchinson as 'a Derbyshire man, who was a very godly, honest, country gentleman, but had not many things requisite to a great soldier'. The regiments other known officers were Captains Wright, Pendock, Palmer and Creed. One interesting character in the regiment was Quartermaster Richard Franck who was a keen angler and would later to write a book on Scotland. Franck enjoyed the scenery but hated the food, describing the Scottish cooking as 'mere sluttery'.[5]

The part regiment of horse which was active in the Preston campaign was that of colonel Adrian Scroope. Scroope himself was in the west country and Kent during 1648, but a three troop strong detachment under Major Barton was involved. Two companies of Okey's dragoon regiment were also in the Preston campaign and it seems to have become common practice by this time to deploy detachments of the regiment throughout the country to act as scouts

Colonel John Okey, from a nineteenth century copy of a contemporary print. Men of Okey's regiment fought on both sides at Preston, though the Colonel himself, who missed the battle, was a staunch member of the New Model. He was eventually executed as a regicide at Tyburn in 1662.

and skirmishers. Colonel John Okey fought in Wales in 1648, but later in the year was with another detachment in the south whilst about 200 of his men fought at Preston. Interestingly, Okey's dragoons were one of the very few parliamentarian units to suffer any serious defection to the enemy. Early in 1648 captain Edward Wogan and his company had defected to the Scots. Men of Okey's regiment would therefore fight on both sides.

Four regiments of New Model foot were at Preston. Best known of these was Lord Fairfax's own, founded in early 1645 and incorporating men from the Eastern Association. The regiment fought well at Naseby, but refused to go to Ireland in 1647 before its arrears had been paid and Captain White appears to have been the main instigator of this insubordination. By the end of the year many of the unit's old officers had been replaced. Since Fairfax himself was not leading his regiment it was commanded during the Preston campaign by Lieutenant Colonel William Cowell. Remarkably White was now major and the captains are thought to have been Priest, Pitson, Keane, Baldwin, Bolton, Leigh and Farley.

Overton's regiment of foot was under the colonelship of Robert Overton, a distinguished soldier, though not present at Preston because he had recently been appointed deputy governor of Hull. In his absence Lieutenant Colonel Thomas Reade commanded the six companies of the regiment involved in the campaign. Since Overton was not there Cromwell usually referred to the unit as 'Reade's'. Reade was related by marriage to both the Winthrop family and the army chaplain, Hugh Peters. The regiment's major was a man called Wade and the captains were Knowles, Gough, Hughes, Reade and Orpin.

Colonel Richard Deane of Gloucestershire led his own regiment at Preston. Deane had served in the parliamentary artillery during the first war and was in fact the regiment's second colonel having succeeded Thomas Rainborowe

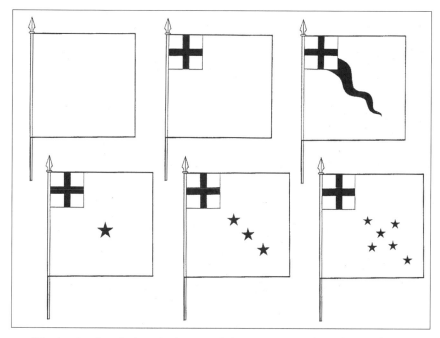

The 'ensigns' or 'colours' of some of the companies of Fairfax's infantry regiment of the New Model Army. The background colour or 'field' of this regiment was green; individual companies were distinguished by the addition of St. George cross, and greater or lesser numbers of symbols or 'differences'. Similar systems were applied to the colours of many of the infantry regiments.

in 1647. Few of Deane's officers are yet identified, but captain Flower was wounded fighting at Pembroke, and Captain Walker and Lieutenant Shipman are believed to have been at Preston.

Pride's regiment completed the New Model complement at Preston. Pride had started off as a captain in the Earl of Essex's army before going to the new regiment in 1645. The unit was at that time commanded by Edward Harley and saw hard service in the west country at the end of the First Civil War, as well as being present at Naseby. Pride, who had already been promoted to lieutenant colonel, was finally given the colonelcy during the disturbances of 1647 when a petition to parliament had led to Harley's impeachment. Pride's lieutenant colonel was William Goffe and his original major George Gregson; Gregson was, however, wounded at Chepstow and replaced by captain Mason. Captains Sakill and Hawes are also thought to have been at Preston.[6]

A vital supplement to the New Model were the regiments of the 'Northern Association'. Formed during the First Civil War, the Association troops, which were primarily from Yorkshire, were locally funded and administered. Major General John Lambert, native of Calton in Malhamdale, had first served with

Major General John Lambert, commander of the parliamentarian Northern Association army, pictured *c.* 1650. (*National Portrait Gallery*)

the Northern Association in 1642 as a humble cornet of horse, aged only 23. Within two years he had risen to the rank of colonel and was in command of his own regiment of dragoons. In 1644 he was at Marston Moor and in 1645 was appointed commissary general. He was, however, defeated by Marmaduke Langdale and was wounded. Lambert then went to fight in the New Model, but was appointed to lead the Northern Association in July 1647, when General Sydenham Poyntz made clear his intention to side with parliament against the army, and the Northern Association mutinied. During this period Lambert became clearly associated with the 'Independents' and appears to have assisted Henry Ireton in the drawing up of the 'Declaration of the Armey'.

His reputation was always one of a tact, subtlety and honesty, which belied his tender years. Cromwell came to refer to him either as 'honest John', or 'bottomless Lambert', the latter in reference to his deep, often unfathomable, nature. In the autumn of 1647, despite reductions in the army, Lambert was able to reimpose order and reorganise pay and billeting. He was prepared to use courts martial and harsh punishment, but in the words of one observer,

> Such fairness, civility and moderation doth he use, moving equally to all according to justice, and endeavouring, now the sword is sheathed, to win and overcome by love . . . A man so completely composed for such employ-ment could not have been pitched upon besides.

By the time of Preston the Northern Association regiments would be little, if at all, inferior to the New Model, and had the advantage that they were possessed of good local intelligence. In terms of weaknesses there were really only two: in order to lessen the burdens of pay and billeting the troops were spread very thin, and they were painfully few in number.

Lambert's own regiment of horse had very probably been commanded by Poyntz until 1647. It was well disciplined and its most important officers are known: the lieutenant colonel was Goodrich, and the remaining troop commanders were Major Rokeby and Captains Baines, Pockley and Stoddart. The Quartermaster was a tough character called Diamond who later distin-guished himself in a particularly nasty brawl near Edinburgh. The other Northern Association horse regiment which served at Preston was Robert Lilburne's. Formed in Durham in 1644 it was kept up to strength whilst others were allowed to dwindle. In September 1647 it was involved in a policing operation against the thieving 'moss troopers' of Northumberland. From Lilburne's would come some of the outstanding characters of the Preston campaign. Major John Sanderson, who seems to have served, officially or unofficially, as scoutmaster, Major Smithson and Captains Lilburne, Wilkin-son and Bradford. Judging from the eyewitness accounts Lilburne's regiment often served in a scouting or skirmishing capacity, a role in which they excelled.[7]

The Northern Association's only foot regiment at Preston was led by York-shire colonel John Bright. Remarkably he had also raised the regiment himself, in 1643, at which time he was only 24 years old. The unit fought well in the First Civil War, including Marston Moor. In the words of Captain John Hodgson of the regiment, 'he was but young when he first had the command, but he grew very valiant and prudent, and had his officers and soldiers under good conduct'. Bright's major was the energetic Pownall, whose scouting and skirmishing skills would prove exceptionally useful.

The third pillar of the parliamentarian army during the campaign was the county militias, most outstandingly that of Lancashire which provided about a quarter of Cromwell's force at Preston. If the New Model was the latest development, then the militia was almost the most ancient of organisations in England. In theory, and with few exceptions, all males between 16 and 60 were liable for militia service. In practice only a proportion were selected and trained, this relatively small part often being known as the 'trained bands'. When required the monarch would order an army to be raised from the militias; his chief officer in each county for this purpose was the lord lieutenant, who in his turn would pass work on to his deputies. Very often, if the force remained in England, it would remain locally funded and administered.

During the reign of Elizabeth I the system was relatively little used save in times of emergency, but under the early Stuarts there were efforts to reform and make the mechanism more effective. 'Musters' of the militia were held more frequently with specialist 'muster masters' appointed, drill books standardised, and on at least one occasion experienced non commissioned officers were brought in from the Low Countries to drill the troops. King Charles' attempts to create an 'exact militia' and his power to raise armies under 'Commissions of Array' would themselves eventually turn into grievances of parliament against the king. When civil war came parliament would itself call out the troops under a rival 'militia ordinance'.[8]

County troops were probably not quite as experienced as the New Model, but the qualitative difference may not have been as great as is sometimes suggested. In Lancashire the parliamentarian forces had seen a good deal of action, much of it in sieges and skirmishes, but also in battle at Whalley in 1643 where the Earl of Derby had suffered a considerable reverse. The Lancashiremen were also fighting under known and experienced local commanders. Foremost amongst these was Colonel Ralph Ashton (or 'Assheton'), a veteran of the First Civil War whose battle honours included the defence of Bolton, the sieges of Chester, York, Lathom House and Hornby Castle, as well as pitched battle at Adwalton and a successful campaign in the Fylde. He was appointed commander in chief in Lancashire in May 1648. By June he had succeeded in raising, or perhaps resurrecting, four regiments of foot and two of horse.

The colonels of these regiments were of scarcely less calibre than their chief. Colonel Alexander Rigby, second in command, and with his own cavalry regiment, had a similar pedigree. He had been a determined parliamentarian since at least 1642, and as member for Preston had been one of those who prepared the impeachment of the Earl of Derby. In October of that year Rigby had been appointed colonel for Amounderness and Leyland hundreds; his campaigns included two sieges of Lathom and the defence of Bolton. If not always successful he had displayed considerable resilience and tenacity. He was first to gather forces against the Scottish menace, even before orders had arrived. Colonel Dodding was also a long-term parliamentarian; although captured by Lord Derby in 1643 he was soon back in the service of parliament. He was notably successful in the skirmish at Walton, and slow but ultimately successful in the siege of Greenhalgh castle at Garstang.

Ughtred Shuttleworth was perhaps the least-known quantity amongst the Lancashire colonels. Whilst he was a member of the staunchly parliamentarian Shuttleworth family, which had fought against the king during the First Civil War, he was a convinced Presbyterian and political moderate, highly suspicious of the New Model, the 'Independents' and further change. Very likely he was one of the prime movers behind the 'declaration' to parliament of 9 May 1648, and certainly a signatory to the letter which accompanied it. The main point of the declaration was that the writers wanted a settled 'regular' government, under king as well as parliament. The letter went further:

> Our soldiery apprehend themselves in great straits; for if the army come down, and they join with them to suppress the Cavaliers, they fear and are very jealous that the army will afterwards fall upon them and suppress them.[9]

With hindsight one can see that these fears were grounded, if not even partially self-fulfilling. Cromwell would certainly have known of this sentiment, and it may have been one of the reasons which led him to put the Lancashire regiments in the second line at Preston. Assessing troop quality is always difficult, but from contemporary evidence it is difficult to escape the conclusion that the Lancashire county regiments were at least fair. According to one contemporary pamphlet the common soldiers of Lancashire were 'exceeding forward to fight the enemy'. Captain Hodgson who met them first hand, and as a Yorkshireman probably had little predisposition to be biased in their favour, wrote:

> The Lancashire foot were as stout men as were in the world, and as brave firemen [musketeers]. I have often told them they were as good fighters, and as great plunderers, as ever went to a field.[10]

Perhaps the Lancashire regiments only really had two significant weaknesses. One was relative lack of numbers, and Hodgson seems to have treated them as if all their infantry were really only one unit, whilst Cromwell's statistics suggest that their foot cannot much have exceeded 350 per regiment. The other drawback was their inherent localism; they would fight well and with the added advantage of local knowledge within their county, but they would not go far beyond it. In the First Civil War Lancashire militia had campaigned in Yorkshire and Cheshire but this seems to have been the limit of their sphere of operations. Outside this theatre the troops of other counties would have to be used.

Scottish and royalists

Scottish armies of the civil war period had a reputation for hardiness and an ability to operate in inhospitable terrain. In the Bishop's War of 1640 the Scots inflicted an humiliating defeat on a traditionally raised and poorly motivated English army. From the end of 1643 they were in alliance with parliament in the First Civil War, as signatories to the 'Solemn League and Covenant'. At Marston Moor they provided vital numbers of men and field guns, which in co-operation with the Eastern and Northern Association armies, tipped the balance against the King in the north. Later the 'Covenanters' fought a war on two fronts, with the English parliamentarians against royalist strongholds like Newark; and a less successful civil war of their own with the royalist Earl of Montrose.

Given the relative size of the Scottish kingdom their infantry was numerous and reasonably well trained. Many Scots had fought abroad in the Thirty Years War, as complete units or individual soldiers of fortune. There were 'highland' units in the Scottish forces and an historic attachment to the basket hilted broadsword, but their main strength lay, like most other armies of the period, in conventionally-organised regiments of pikemen and musketeers. Similarly most Scottish troops did not wear the kilt but were usually distinguished by 'hodden grey' jackets and blue cloth bonnets. Like the Swiss in the previous century they had a reputation as mercenaries, and some officers were already involved in the English civil wars before Scottish participation became official policy. The Scottish armies were generally well provided with artillery, and specialised in light, short-range guns which were easier to manoeuvre over bad country. Cavalry tended to be a weaker arm, perhaps because horses bred for the mountains and moors were less suited to the open battlefield, or perhaps because the Scottish horse was not usually deployed as a battle winning force.

Following the cessation of hostilities in the First Civil War the Scottish army had returned home and was itself remodelled into a force of 6,000 foot and 1,200 horse. This body would provide the starting point for raising the much larger 'Engager' army which would invade England in 1648. The decision to invade in support of Charles I was less than unanimous, the Scottish parliament voting by a majority of 30 in favour of the enterprise, and there were significant objectors. Whilst the nobility and gentry of Scotland broadly supported the

The Duke of
Hamilton, after
Van Dyke,
pictured in the
1630s.

engagement, the Kirk and the Earl of Argyle were against it. Former generals
Alexander and David Leslie would not serve with the new army, and the leader
of the Engager forces would be James Duke of Hamilton.

Hamilton was very much a nobleman and politician as well as a soldier. He
was born in 1606 and, having attended Oxford, inherited his titles from his
late father in 1625. As a courtier to the house of Stuart he was both a gentleman
of the bedchamber and a privy councillor. In 1630 he was granted permission

to raise an expedition to go to the aid of Gustavus Adolphus in Germany. The result was less than spectacular; recruitment was slow and enemies spread the rumour that his soldiers were intended for a coup in Scotland rather than campaign on the continent. When his force did finally land in Germany it was used for garrisoning forts on the Oder and for the blockade of Magdeburg.

Hamilton remained popular with Charles I and was granted various favours and monopolies in the 1630s. During the crisis between the king and Scotland in 1638–40 he remained loyal to Charles and was made a royal commissioner. When negotiation failed he was created a general, but this military interlude was to prove less fruitful than the last, being dogged by changes of plan and mutinies. Ultimately Hamilton had little to gain and much to lose as he had property and interests both sides of the border. He concluded by trying to placate all parties, including the new 'Long' parliament in England in 1641. Unfortunately, one person he left completely alienated was the Marquis of

A contemporary woodcut of Lieutenant General James Livingstone, Earl of Callander. Though an experienced soldier he did not work well with the Duke of Hamilton.

Montrose, who at least on the face of it should have been a natural ally against the Covenanters.

Hamilton and his brother were forced to abandon Scotland and flee to Oxford. Having now demonstrated his potential for ingratiating himself with the king's enemies Charles' advisors prevailed upon him to have Hamilton arrested. He spent more than a year imprisoned in Cornwall before being released and making his way back to Scotland after the war.[11]

James Livingstone, Earl of Callander, was appointed lieutenant general and second in command of the engager army. Callander was a younger son of the Earl of Linlithgow who had purchased a barony in 1634. Unlike Hamilton he was a career soldier, as one account put it, he

> was bred from his youth a soldier in the wars of Germany and the Low Countries, where he long commanded a regiment of Scottish foot, and had gained (deservedly) the reputation of a man of great courage; and understood well the Dutch discipline of war, which he observed with a strictness that seemed not free of affectation.[12]

In 1640 he was second in command to General Leslie fighting against the English in the successful Second Bishop's War. During the First Civil War he served in the army of the Solemn League and Covenant against the king, but his detractors argued that he was promoted beyond his ability and was prone to factionalism. It was certainly true that he did not work well under Hamilton.

John, Earl of Middleton, was to be lieutenant general of the Horse. Like Callander he was an experienced soldier and had begun at the ground floor of the profession, trailing a pike in Hepburn's regiment in the French service. He fought in England for parliament during the First Civil War and was a lieutenant general until the army was new modelled. According to Burnet Middleton enjoyed Hamilton's confidence, being a man of much 'courage and honour'.

Lieutenant general of foot was William Baillie, another experienced soldier. In the Thirty Years War in Europe he fought under Gustavus and became colonel of a Dutch foot regiment. Returning to Scotland in 1638 his experience was soon put to good use; he served under Leslie and Leven in 1639 and 1640, and took an important role in England in 1644 when he was present at Marston Moor. The next year he fought against the Montrose in the highlands, but this campaign was a disaster.

If Callander was a dubious choice and Baillie was not universally successful, Sir James Turner, the army's adjutant general, would do little to heal any disagreement. Bishop Burnet described him as 'naturally fierce' but mad when drunk, 'and that was very often'. Turner had been born in 1615 and graduated from Glasgow university in 1631. He clearly fancied himself a military theorist, and whilst partly bluster he did have a good deal of experience. He first served on the continent in 1632 when he promptly succumbed to a camp fever and was for six weeks unable to walk. Until 1640 he served intermittently in Denmark and Germany, learned enough German to make sense of the various schools of war, was present at several battles and suffered another debilitating bout of fever which laid him low for 17 weeks.[13]

Organising the Scottish army for campaign was no easy matter. May 21 1648 was appointed as the day for the rendezvous of the shire levies and there was immediate complaint that this was an impossibly tight schedule, both from the Kirk and some of the shires. In Clydesdale there was active resistance, begun apparently by a small band of draft dodgers and deserters who fled to Loudon Hill. Later a body of dissenters, believed to total over 1,000, gathered at Mauchline Moor and was met by generals Middleton and Callander at the head of a force of 2,300. Negotiation commenced and some of the crowd dispersed, but the hard core rebels required a cavalry charge from Middleton's troopers to convince them. Forty of the dissidents were killed, but not before Middleton had suffered a minor wound, inflicted it was said, by a blacksmith.

In the face of these problems stern measures were required to make sure that the will of the Scottish parliament was enforced. Various officials, magistrates and town councillors who had been dragging their heels, or 'professed scruple of conscience' against the levy, were barred from their positions or thrown into the 'tollbooth' for a few days to reconsider. Another method of coercion practised was to billet troops on the backsliders. Sir James Turner was one of the main proponents of this method which he used in the Glasgow area, 'the quartering of tuo or three troopers, and halfe a dozen musketeers was ane argument strong enough, in tuo or three nights time, to make the hardest headed Covenanter in the toune to forsake the kirk, and side with the parliament'.

Exactly how many soldiers were raised remains open to question. The most optimistic figure banded about was in excess of 40,000, but this can never really have been a practical proposition, especially bearing in mind that the Scottish invasion force of 1640 had been a little under 20,000 and that of 1644 a little over that figure. On 21 May the Scottish parliament had set the strength of the new army at 30,000 foot and 6,000 horse, but as will be seen what was achieved was a good deal less. Sir James Turner described the regiments marching from Scotland as 'halfe of their numbers they sould have beene' and undisciplined.

General Lambert who was possessed of some of the best intelligence of the campaign reported, just prior to the Scottish invasion, that their army was 14,000 in immediate readiness in Dumfries, plus a further 3,000 expected. It seems reasonable to suggest that Hamilton's army may have numbered as much as 18,000 at the outset and fewer at Preston. Cromwell's estimation was that the Scottish army totalled 12,000 foot and 5,000 horse in mid August, whilst Scottish sources protested that the true figure was less. Turner put the whole at 14,000, and Bishop Burnet would later concur stating that the infantry were 10,000 the horse 4,000. Doubtless the precise number was somewhere between 14,000 and 17,000 and an attempt has been made elsewhere to justify an approximate total of 15,000, not including Munro's contingent.[14]

The quality of the Engager army of 1648 is also a matter of debate, but one factor more than any other appears to have undermined their efficiency, and that was supply. Billeting troops on civilians was a double-edged sword within Scotland because whilst it may have had a coercive effect in the short term it was not likely to endear the engager cause to the public later on. Within England plundering would be rife, perhaps not only through ill discipline, but because it was necessary to feed the troops. Any lingering doubts that Lancashire Presbyterians and moderates had about helping Cromwell to beat the Scots would very quickly be dispelled, as the Scots took away the very 'crocks and pot hooks', drove with them their victim's sheep and horses, and abused the locals both male and female.[15]

Most sources agree that the Scottish horse and foot were reasonably well armed, but the level of training is likely to have varied. A number of regiments had been kept in being, prior to 1648, as a standing army, and it is difficult to believe that these were not largely composed of veterans. Similarly it is likely that a proportion of the rank and file had, like their senior officers, experience of foreign service. Where there was a lack of skill it was probably amongst the newly levied, and sometimes unwilling, who had been raised in May and June 1648. There would be some at Preston who had only two months experience and it was these who were most fitting of Turner's epithets regarding 'raw' troops.

Scottish organisation was rather different to their opponents. Cavalry regiments were intended to be 180 men in three troops; even at full strength this made them only half the size of a cavalry regiment in the English New Model, and it also meant that there were proportionately many more colonels. Handling such a force effectively would have been a difficult task. Another difference was that the Scottish cavalry often wielded the lance, a potent weapon when properly used, especially against disorganised foot soldiers. Scottish infantry regiments also varied in size, many were notionally 800 in strength, others even more, but in practice most were smaller. It seems likely that the average strength at Preston was between 400 and 600.

Amongst the infantry regiments at least four dated back to the standing army which had existed prior to 1648. Argyle's regiment is thought to have been particularly weak, due to the fact that its colonel did not approve of the

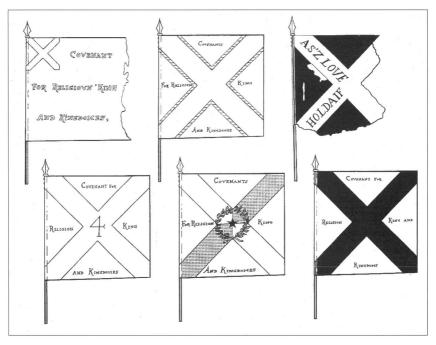

Scottish colours (1). Many of the Scottish colours from the Preston campaign were meticulously recorded in a manuscript by Payne Fisher, now known as British Library harl. 1460. Those shown here are: top left, one of the Drummond's regiment, with blue field and white saltire; top centre, one from Atholl's regiment with a white saltire edged in red on a blue field; top right, one from Kieth's regiment with a red field and large white saltire and red lettering; bottom left, one of Home's regiment with a green field, white saltire, and black Arabic numeral '4'; bottom centre, an example from Baillie's regiment with a blue field, yellow and white saltire; companies in Baillie's were apparently distinguished by the number of stars; bottom right a colour from Kellie's regiment, with red saltire on yellow field.

enterprise. The General of the Artillery's regiment was nominally 800, but since one of the companies numbered only 60 it was perhaps 500 all told. Turner's regiment, formally Holburn's Lowland regiment, and Baillie's own regiment were also supposed to be 800, but again were probably weaker.

The other infantry regiments presented considerable variations in strength and quality. The biggest and most potent units are likely to have been Hamilton and Callander's own, the former with a notional strength of 1,500. At the other end of the scale was Frazer's Firelocks; although probably competent troops, and armed with modern firelocks rather than the matchlock musket, there is no reason to suppose that they numbered more than a few companies. Their most likely employment would have been as artillery guards or as skirmishers.[16]

Scottish colours (2). A further selection indicating the variety among the flags of the Scottish infantry. Top left, a colour of Tullibardine's, with a white field, red saltire, and black lettering; top centre, one from Turner's regiment with the classic white saltire on blue ground; Top right a colour from Bargany's regiment, with blue field, white saltire, and green wreath, companies distinguished by stars; bottom left, one from Frazer's 'firelocks', possibly that of captain Leslie, with white saltire, blue ground and bronze coloured vessel with green foliage; bottom centre, the tattered colour of captain Erskine's company of Keiths regiment with red ground, white saltire, and a sword arm motif. Bottom right, a striking colour from Argyle's regiment, with black field and yellow saltire.

Most modern accounts of the Battle of Preston state that the Scottish army had no artillery in the campaign. The sole justification for this point of view seems to be the famous statement in Turner's memoirs regarding Alexander Hamilton, the General of Artillery:

we had no cannon, nay not one field peece, very litle amunition, and not one officer to direct it. Deare Sandie being groune old and doated, had given no fitting orders for these things.

It is remarkable therefore that two contemporary tracts describe the capture of Scottish guns at Preston, and that an eighteenth-century account mentions their use. It is all the more surprising since most Scottish armies of the period seem to have had even more artillery than their English equivalents.[17]

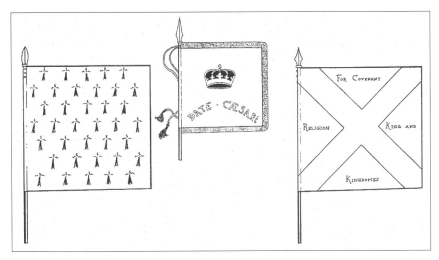

Scottish colours from the Duke of Hamilton's own regiments (3). Left,
Colonel's colour Hamilton's infantry regiment; centre' cornet of Hamilton's
Horse with blue field, gold lettering and fringe, gold and red coronet; and right
another of Hamilton's infantry colours with black field and white saltire.

Such contradictions are not easily explained, but it is possible that, even
though there was no formal 'train' of artillery and no siege guns, some units
brought their own light pieces with them. Maybe Turner's own regiment had
no such provision, or alternately he did not regard light 'leather guns' or
'frames' as either proper cannon or 'field guns'.

An interesting addition to the main Scottish army was the so called 'New
Scots' force brought over from Ireland to support the royalist cause under
Major General George Munro. The Scots had maintained an army in Ulster
since 1642, prompted by the bloody rebellion of the previous year. This force,
nominally 10,000 strong at the outset, was tasked with the maintenance of the
'Protestant interest'; by 1647 it had seen several campaigns, but its pay was
long in arrears. Since the English had guaranteed their pay these troops would
have a pecuniary interest in the victory of Hamilton and the English royalists.
Three Scottish commissioners, Sir James Macdougal, Sir William Cocherane
and Mr Alexander Crawford, therefore went to Ulster to arrange the transfer
of troops to Scotland in support of Hamilton. They promised a month's pay
to expedite matters, half before, and half after arrival in Scotland. English
representatives did their best to scupper the deal, but their eleventh hour
intercessions were too late to be convincing.

The exact composition of Munro's army is unclear, although it was apparently intended to number 1,200 horse and 2,100 foot. The horse were organised
in 12 troops, the foot were drawn from six regiments and are said to have been
in 36 companies. In the event less than 3,000 made it to join the invasion, 300

men of Dalyell's regiment being taken prisoner by parliamentarian warships in July as they attempted to cross to Galloway in small boats. Turner gave the even smaller figure of 1,500 foot and 300 horse for Monro's command, but this appears to have been something of an under estimate because even after the campaign his returns show at least 362 horse and 1,099 foot. Cromwell in his dispatches assumed Monro's strength at 2,700 and called them a 'considerable force'. Though veterans Munro's army did have a weakness, and this was that their commander regarded them as separate and distinct from the Scottish army proper. Since commissioners had negotiated for his participation Munro was not about to allow his command to be subsumed within Hamilton's army; throughout the campaign they would operate as an independent unit.[18]

The royalists in northern England had one of the most difficult recruiting jobs of 1648. Forces had to be prepared in the face of parliamentarian opposition, as far as possible in concert with their Scottish allies, and in such a way as to get regiments into being without immediately falling victim to local parliamentarian armies. War weariness was a distinct obstacle as many potential recruits had lately fought for the king in a four year war, and many had formally made their peace with their enemies. Luckily there were a handful of loyal veteran royalists around with which to build such an army, and enough other distractions for the New Model to make it possible.

From the point of view of the Battle of Preston the most important of these veterans was Marmaduke, Lord Langdale. Born in 1598 he was a Catholic and the son of Peter Langdale, of Beverley, Yorkshire. In the Thirty Years War he served in Europe on behalf of the Queen of Bohemia, returning to England some time in the 1630s. In 1639 he was made High Sheriff of Yorkshire but despite this appointment was reluctant to collect the 'ship money' tax on the king's behalf. Although he may have had reservations about some aspects of the 'Personal Rule' of Charles I, his heart was for the king and he was made a

The English royalist General Marmaduke Lord Langdale, able commander of the 'Northern Horse' during the First Civil War.

'Commissioner of Array' in July 1642. Soon after he was a royalist colonel, seeing much active service in 1643 and 1644, eventually commanding a whole cavalry brigade known as the 'Northern Horse'. He fought at Marston Moor, Naseby, Donnington, Melton Mowbray and many minor actions, before escaping to the Isle of Man late in 1645. According to Sir Henry Slingsby, Langdale was a 'caesar', who was 'severe and precise in exacting of discipline', a man not afraid to lead from the front and by personal example. Clearly an able commander he was nonetheless criticised by Clarendon for what he perceived as pride and arrogance.[19]

Another important figure was Sir Philip Musgrave. A few years younger than Langdale, Musgrave had served as a member for Westmorland in both the 'short' and 'long' parliaments. His biographer, clergyman Gilbert Burton, described him as of 'a melancholly disposition and weak body'. If this were true he was also a man of great determination, for apart from serving as a deputy lieutenant he was a colonel in the trained bands formed to fight the Scots in 1639 and 1640, and a 'Commissioner of Array' for the king two years later. He defended Carlisle and in 1645 fought with the main royalist army, being captured at Rowton Heath that September.

The last of the 'big three' northern royalists to have a bearing on the fight at Preston was Sir Thomas Tyldesley, known to some as 'the finest knight in England'. Born in 1612, of Anglo-Catholic parents, he is thought to have had some experience of foreign service, but returned to his native Lancashire by 1634. He raised forces for the king at the outbreak of the First Civil War and was lieutenant colonel to Lord Molyneux at Edgehill. The next year he took to the field with his own regiments of horse and foot and campaigned widely in Yorkshire, Lancashire and the south. He fought at Marston Moor in 1644, where he appears to have led a brigade rather than just one regiment. Captured at Montgomery later that year, he was a prisoner for sometime before escaping from Stafford castle in 1645. In 1646 he defended Lichfield and, when finally ordered to capitulate by the king, escaped to the Isle of Man.

As far as can be determined the northern English royalists succeeded in raising about 5,000 men in 1648, the majority of whom fought at Preston. The most significant absence was Tyldesley's regiment which, at the time of the battle, was besieging Lancaster. Those involved in the battle totalled about 3,000 foot and 700 horse, and were divided into eight foot regiments and a similar number of troops of horse raised by the colonels of the foot regiments. Assuming that the foot were roughly equally divided, each of the royalist foot regiments would have been about 375 men, a similar strength to most of the Scottish and Lancashire militia regiments, but considerably weaker than the foot of the English New Model.

The regimental colonels, apart from Sir Philip Musgrave, were Sir Edward

Musgrave, Sir Henry Bellingham, Sir Patricius Curwen, Sir William Huddlestone, Sir Henry Featherstone, William Carleton and Henry Chator.

Sir Edward Musgrave, who had been born in 1621, was a Cumberland man and had been Sheriff of that county during the First Civil War, and had also served under the Earl of Newcastle. Bellingham, a native of Westmorland, was a much older man, being about fifty at the time of the battle. He had a legal background, and had served as MP for his county. Bellingham has been described as a 'reluctant field officer', but nonetheless had received his commission from the Earl of Newcastle as early as 1643, and certainly raised troops for the King in Cumberland in 1644. He was related, by marriage, to the Curwen family.

Sir Patricius Curwen, in his mid forties in 1648, was a Justice of the Peace, Deputy Lieutenant and Sheriff for Cumberland. He was also an MP before the war and, after 1642, sat in the rival royalist parliament set up by Charles I at Oxford. He was commissioned to raise a regiment in 1643. It has been suggested that Curwen was no friend to Sir Philip Musgrave, whose authority he resented, and if so it was perhaps a good thing for the royalist efforts at Preston that Curwen did not have to fight under his command. Sir William Huddlestone, also from Cumberland, was another long term royalist, and one with a wealth of experience on the battlefield. He was born about 1605, and in 1639 and 1640 he had served as a captain in the English army during the disastrous 'Bishop's Wars'. He had been a member of the royalist Commission of Array in 1642, and some sources suggest that he fought at Edgehill. In 1644 he had campaigned against the Scots in Durham and was at Marston Moor that July.

Less is known of Sir Henry Featherstone, but he may be synonymous with the Henry Featherstonhaugh who had served as a Major under Colonel Sir Richard Dacre of Cumberland. If so he was one of the youngest colonels present at Preston, being only 24 years old at the time. William Carlton was born in 1607 and had previous military experience serving under Sir Henry Fletcher as lieutenant colonel in earlier campaigns. Henry Chator, or 'Chaytor', later to be described by the Earl of Buckingham as 'a brave and discreet officer', was a Yorkshireman who had already seen long service by 1648, although his exact age is uncertain. A lieutenant in the army serving against the Scots in 1640, he had also fought in Ireland and it seems that this previous experience had influenced the Earl of Newcastle to promote him direct to colonel during the First Civil War. He was doubtless a natural choice for command during the Second Civil War.

There were also other personalities of note with Langdale's army, one such being Sir Lewis Dyves. Dyves had held the appointment of Governor of Abingdon, and later Governor of Sherborne, in the First Civil War, and had also commanded regiments of his own; in the second he was to serve the sometimes frustrating post of liaison officer with the Scots.[20]

Other officers included Lieutenant Colonel John Galliard, a foreign national who had served in Langdale's northern horse, and Lieutenant Colonel Ferdinando Huddlestone of Sir Philip Musgrave's regiment, and son to Sir William Huddlestone. Also Lieutenant Colonel Edward Hutchinson, previously of Pennyman's regiment, Colonel William Owen who had also seen extensive service, and Major David Errington. Most of Langdale's officers were therefore well experienced and it is likely that the same went for at least a proportion of the rank and file. From the stout performance of Langdale's army at Preston it may be surmised that it was little inferior to that of Cromwell.

It is likely, however, that the royalists would have had greater problems with arms and supplies. This is well illustrated by the case of the Yorkshire colonel Arthur Redhead, who imported arms for the campaign from abroad, a fact that did not go unnoticed by local parliamentarians. Colonel Edward Grey of Chillingham in Northumberland was suspected even before he made a move. In July 1648 Sir Arthur Heselrig reported him to parliament as an 'active and dangerous' man, who had committed more 'mischief' in the royalist cause than any in the north and was best placed under local arrest.[21]

Some of the potential difficulties of cooperation with the Scots were highlighted by Sir Philip Musgrave's own 'relation'. About March 1648 both he and Langdale had travelled to Edinburgh, having heard from Scottish agents that a plan for invasion in support of the king was well advanced. They found that not only were preparations far from complete, but that Lord Lannark was embarrassed by their presence. They were forced to keep to their lodgings whilst the Scottish leaders would visit them conspiratorially at night. Commissioners from the English Parliament who were still in town in the meantime demanded that Musgrave and Sir Thomas Glenham, another prominent royalist, should be handed over.

By 27 April they had succeeded only in securing the less than generous arrangement that Langdale would secure Berwick and Carlisle, on the understanding that they would be handed over to the Scots on demand. Though the Scots did not promise publicly to endorse the English royalists' actions, they did offer 500 muskets and 10 barrels of powder to each garrison. Once the coups in Berwick and Carlisle were complete the Scots undertook to enter England within 20 days, and to relieve them immediately if threatened. According to Musgrave's version of the secret negotiations the Scots were definitely senior partners in the enterprise, but the exact timing of the taking of the border towns was not stipulated.[22]

3

The Coming of the Second Civil War

HARLES I AND HIS PARLIAMENT had gone to war in 1642 over power, religion and money; the 'English' Civil War had been just a part of a wider conflict which took in Scotland, Ireland and Wales. When the 'Great' or First Civil War came to an end in 1646 the king had been militarily defeated, but though a prisoner he was still king, and the major constitutional issues remained unresolved. Undoubtedly Charles still believed in his God-given right to rule and there was still a strong body of moderates in parliament who surmised that any durable solution would have to involve the king. Many indeed had fought the war under colour that they supported 'King and Parliament', not the parliament against the king. In the eyes of such men recourse to arms had only been necessary because his majesty was in the thrall of cavalier 'malignants' and papists. The war was therefore to 'restore' the ancient rights of Englishmen, as granted by Magna Carta, and not to promote a complete overturning of the political structures of England. As early as the autumn of 1644 there were signs of stress within the parliamentarian alliance. There were those who wanted the war prosecuted with the utmost vigour, by a new and more professional army; there were those prepared for compromise; and there were those, like the Scots, who had an entirely different agenda.[1]

Charles had first surrendered to the Scots, at Newark, in May 1646. Since Marston Moor almost two years previously it had become increasingly unlikely that he would win the war, and the unlikelihood had become a near certainty after Naseby in June 1645. The decision to surrender to the Scots was itself a gambit, designed to secure the best terms and split the erstwhile allies. Scotland and parliament had been in alliance for over two years under the terms of the 'Solemn League and Covenant', but with the fighting all but over the raison d'etre of the entente was wearing thin. In the summer after his capture Charles was presented with the 'Newcastle Propositions', which, amongst other things,

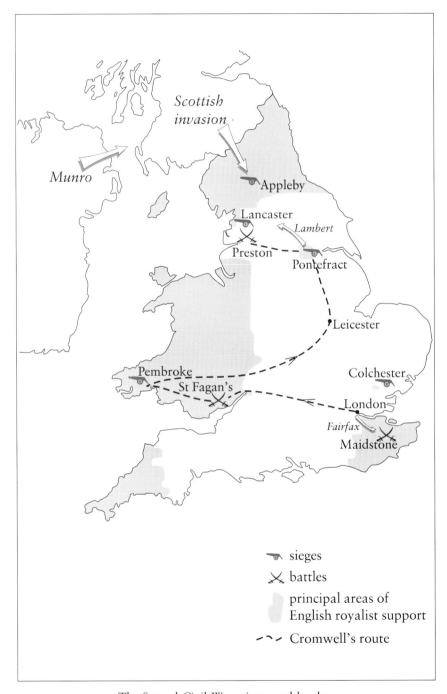

The Second Civil War: sieges and battles.

suggested a Presbyterian church for England and the exclusion of ex-royalists from public life. Even as he considered these relatively mild, but unpalatable, terms the Scots came to a financial settlement with the parliament concerning their participation in the late war and their occupation of Northumberland. They were paid £400,000 to vacate English soil, and since the king would not introduce Presbyterianism in England, the obdurate monarch was left behind them when they retired and taken into 'protective' custody at Holdenby House in Northamptonshire. Although the king's person was not explicitly part of the deal, the money was apprehended by royalists as parallel to the biblical betrayal by Judas.

The year 1647 saw further deterioration of the situation. By March army 'arrears', or deficits in pay, to the New Model had reached two and a half million pounds. On the one hand the 'Presbyterian' faction in parliament sought a prompt and moderate settlement with the king, together with the disbandment of the army; on the other the 'Independents' were suspicious of any accommodation with Charles which might undo everything which had been struggled for. One critical observer noted that the officers of the New Model who were once clad in rags, were now arrayed in scarlet, and that the men had forgotten how to obey. The soldiers themselves saw disbandment as at best robbery of the money they were owed, and at worst a blatant attempt at counter revolution.

That summer there were some soldiers who were owed six months pay. On 4 June the king was seized from Holdenby by a detachment under Cornet Joyce, and became a closely guarded political pawn in a new struggle which was emerging between the factions of his opponents. New peace terms were now formulated by the Army Council, and put to the king under the title of the 'Heads of the Proposals'. These were still quite lenient for a party defeated in war, who had already stalled for a year. Charles, inadvisedly, dismissed them out of hand.

Perhaps the king had gambled that dissention between his enemies would finally offer him a way out and indeed the summer of 1647 saw England teeter on the brink of anarchy. The Northern Association Army of Sydenham Poyntz mutinied in July, and this was followed by the second of two bad harvests. There was almost war that year and the new alignment of City, Presbyterians, and London trained bands on the one side, with the bulk of the New Model Army on the other, said much about the way in which the country was beginning to split. Sir Thomas Fairfax, Lord General of the New Model, moved on London and resistance crumbled before there was any fight. When he arrived at the Tower he examined not only the armouries but its records, and on seeing a copy of Magna Carta was moved to comment that it was this 'that which we have fought for and by God's help we must maintain'.

In retrospect the appointment of Major General John Lambert to command the unruly Northern Association forces was little less significant than Fairfax's bloodless subjugation of London. Lambert was aided no doubt in bringing them to heel by the fact that whilst Poyntz was against the 'Independents', his troops had felt common cause with the New Modellers. Exactly what steps Lambert took are recorded in the Order Book of the Council of the Northern Army, a copy of which is preserved at York Minster Library. In councils of war held at Wakefield, Ripon, Knaresborough, and York he dealt systematically with both public grievances against the troops and with the soldiers' own specific problem of pay.

Amongst the soldiers brought to book were a company accused of looting, murderers, drunks and men stealing from those on whom they had been billeted. Several were hung, others cashiered, and some condemned to do public penance, not for political reasons, but for contraventions of the ordinary civil and military laws. At least one case, however, defied all efforts of the council at resolution; Patrick McCourt was accused of both bigamy and murdering his own daughter, whilst in Ireland under arms as a rebel. Lack of evidence precluded a capital solution, but he was whipped and sent to the workhouse for another assault. The officers that sat in the council were drawn from every officer rank, from the major general down to humble cornets, and amongst their names were several who would later distinguish themselves at Preston.

On 10 December 1647 Lambert issued new orders regarding quartering in an effort to make the burdens to the public more equitable. At the same time arrangements for the collection of money from the parishes was improved, with constables being held responsible for the collections of local assessments. The soldiery themselves were only to assist the constable where required, and detailed orders were given regarding their conduct. A list of rates of pay for the Northern Association army accompanied the new instructions.[2]

The grandees of the New Model in the south were also making progress during the autumn of 1647, although here the proceedings took a much more overtly political tone. At the remarkable 'Putney Debates' in late October and early November the army chiefs and representatives of the New Model discussed exactly what it was that would be acceptable as a settlement with their old enemies. 'Levelling' factions within the army called for a significant role in politics and, in the celebrated 'Agreement of the People', a unicameral legislature elected annually. In further debate it emerged that one of the Leveller demands would be for a much wider franchise. At the conclusion Fairfax disowned the Levellers, and in a rendezvous of the army at Corkbush Field, near Ware, matters came to a head when one man was shot for mutiny and others were arrested.[3]

Charles, perhaps sensing that he could make political capital out of his enemies divisions, escaped from Hampton Court: he unerringly jumped from frying pan to fire by surrendering himself to Colonel Hammond at Carisbrook castle on the Isle of Wight. As he explained his position to Sir John Oglander and other gentlemen there,

> I must inform you that, for the preservation of my life, I was forced from Hampton Court. For there were people called Levellers that had both voted and resolved of my death, so that I could no longer dwell there in safety. And, desiring to be somewhat secure till some happy accommodation may be made between me and my Parliament have put myself in this place, for I desire not a drop more of Christian blood should be spilt.[4]

Parliament did try another solution, which was presented to the king in 'Four Bills' at Christmas 1647; he rejected this and negotiations were broken off. Behind the scenes Charles had been preparing another treaty, a secret 'engagement' with the Scots. The leading Scottish 'engagers' were Lords Hamilton, Lanark, Lauderdale and Loudon. The provisions of the agreement committed Charles to the introduction of a Presbyterian church in England and the sending of one of his sons to be resident north of the border. In return the Scots would support him to regain his kingdom. On the face of it this was a better deal than he could expect elsewhere, but there were two awful problems; the New Model Army would not simply disappear, and not all Scots were behind the engagement. Most significantly the Scottish kirk, and Archibald Campbell, the influential Earl of Argyle were against it.[5]

War was now virtually inevitable. Security was closed tighter around the king, and his trusted servants Ashburnham, Berkeley and Legge were barred from him. On 11 April the Scots declared the treaty of 1643, signed between themselves and parliament, at an end. However, though the Scots now began to struggle to raise the necessaries for an army it was to be neither they nor the king who would dictate the pace of events. Rumblings had started in Kent about the new regimes' lack of recognition for Christmas, and there was scattered discontent and demonstrations in Wales, Lancashire and Cheshire.

Though Sir John Owen would stage a minor revolt in north Wales it was south Wales which was the most immediate challenge to authority. In March Colonel John Poyer had refused to disband the Pembroke garrison until it was paid; Chepstow and Tenby followed suit. Colonel Horton, who was sent with a couple of thousand men to restore order, was powerless to do much about the situation. The war of 1648 has been called a 'war of the provinces', and certainly the wave of largely uncoordinated acts which sparked it in different corners of the country posed special difficulties for both sides.

Rumour had now reached parliament that the Scots were raising an army of 40,000 for use against England and swift measures had to be taken to quell unrest in other parts of the Kingdom. Whilst Lord General Fairfax was left to deal with Kent and the south east his second in command, Lieutenant General Oliver Cromwell, was dispatched with a portion of the New Model, perhaps 5,000 strong, to south Wales. He arrived at Chepstow on 11 May to find that the situation was actually improving. Colonel Horton had beaten some of the insurgents in a skirmish at St Fagans three days earlier, and Tenby soon surrendered on the news of Cromwell's arrival.

Pembroke was left as the only significant nut to crack, and Cromwell, writing to William Lenthall, speaker of the House of Commons, from the 'leaguer before Pembroke', was confident of success. He predicted that Poyer's men probably could not survive a fortnight. The only real problem was lack of artillery.

> We have not got our guns and ammunition from Wallingford yet; but, however, we have scraped up a few which stand us in very good stead. Last night we got two little guns planted, which in twenty four hours will take away their mills . . . we made an attempt to storm about ten days since; but our ladders were too short, and the breach so as men could not get over. We lost a few men but I am confident the enemy lost more. Captain Flower of Dean's regiment was wounded; and Major Grigg's Lieutenant and Ensign slain; Captain Burges lies wounded and very sick.[6]

In the meantime the situation in the south east had deteriorated rapidly, but Sir Thomas Fairfax was proving equal to the challenge. He had gathered as many troops as were available on Houndslow heath on 27 May intending to March north, but the Kent royalists were now threatening London from the East and six warships in the Downs had declared for the king. Deal, Sandown and Walmer castles had been seized so Fairfax could no longer afford to leave the area.[7]

4

The Northern Campaign, April to August 1648

Sir Marmaduke Langdale and Sir Philip Musgrave left Scotland, and split up with both hope, and a sense of urgency. As Langdale arrived outside Berwick it became apparent that rumour of the Scottish design was already abroad, and that with only a troop of 100 horse he would have to act immediately. According to one account the mayor had already closed one of the town gates against him, and was preparing to block the other as he arrived. Once safely inside the town he issued a declaration so that his intentions should not be 'misjudged'. His force was there because parliament had failed to bring about a settlement of religion and a well grounded peace; far from disbanding all military forces and including the monarch in the new order a 'schismatical army' had seized and abused the king. Langdale's objectives were to restore the king, ensure the freedom of parliament, disband the armies, uphold the law and preserve the union of England and Scotland.[1]

An urgent message was also sent to Sir Philip Musgrave: since the cat was out of the bag he too would have to act quickly. On 29 April he sent a tiny advanced party of 16 horsemen, led by his kinsman 'Mr Denton', into Carlisle. This little band secured the three gates, imprisoned the mayor, and read out an order in the market place. Obviously the town was sympathetic to the royalist cause, or such a desperate venture would never have succeeded. Musgrave himself rode into Carlisle on 1 May after a gruelling ride in the rain. He found that his 16 stalwarts had swollen to about 150, with '3 great iron gunns' which they had brought five miles to the town. A party of '50 poor ill armed horse but good men' were sent out on patrol from the town, and the parliamentarian Major Chomley retreated out of reach to Appleby.

Sir Philip had acted just in time; Mayor Barwis MP had already called out the Cumberland county militia in the name of parliament, and men were beginning to head for the rendezvous. William Musgrave and 20 royalists met them as they arrived, chasing off the parliamentarian officials, and disarming and dismissing the rank and file as they trickled in. Colonel Wogan, the deserter from Okey's regiment, now arrived from Scotland at the head of his troop. Together they organised the defences of Carlisle, which were manned by 500 men, with sufficient provisions, it was thought, for six months.

On 17 May Langdale arrived in Cumberland, and then marched south via Kendal to Kirby Lonsdale, gathering strength all the time. He had over 1,000 men by the time a rather panicky message was delivered to him from the Scottish command by the hand of Arthur Barclay. On no account was he to engage the enemy until the arrival of the Scottish army. For the next couple of weeks he therefore continued recruiting, and attempted, fruitlessly, to reduce Lancashire by negotiation. The time was not entirely wasted, for by his own estimation his forces at the end of May totalled 3,000 armed foot and 700 poorly armed horse from Cumberland and Westmorland, plus 500 'good horse' who had gathered to his call from other counties. The garrison of Pontefract castle in Yorkshire also declared for the king in early June.[2]

The next news from Scotland was even less promising. Rather than sending reinforcements, or even a morale raising note of congratulation, Langdale was sent letters quizzing the religious affiliations of his men. The Scots were displeased that Langdale was recruiting Catholics, and that his dispatches made no mention of the covenant. In desperation Sir Philip Musgrave was sent back to Edinburgh, 'to endevour a righter understanding' of the proceedings.

Doubtless this move on the part of the Scottish command was designed, at least in part, to appease home critics; but it was also a delaying tactic because their own recruiting was proceeding slowly. On the other hand the Scots had little reason to believe that time was of the essence. Their own limited intelligence suggested that the English parliament and army were hopelessly split, and that the enemy forces were weak and divided. One remarkably optimistic communication to the Earl of Lannark dated 18 April suggested that pro royalist forces in Wales numbered 40,000; that the parliamentary army grandees were considering whether a military occupation of a disaffected London was necessary in the face of the growing unrest in the south east; and that Cornwall was a royalist powerbase. Another letter of the same date suggested that Thornhaugh's regiment were mutinous, marched unwillingly, drank the King's health and wished to disband. Intelligence of early May was unsure whether Cromwell seriously intended to reduce Wales, and whether Scottish intervention would result in a quick victory, or a uniting of Englishmen against them.[3]

In the meantime the parliamentarians were not idle. Major General Lambert had long since returned order to the disaffected within the old parliamentarian Northern Association army, and had begun to take active measures against the royalist forces. At first Lambert kept east of the Pennines, perhaps under the impression that the Scottish attack, when it came, would fall here and push into Yorkshire. This point of view was reinforced by the story circulating at the beginning of June that it was Langdale's intention to march via Kirby Stephen on Yorkshire, catching Lambert before he could concentrate his limited forces. Another apparent indicator was that Langdale dispatched 500 horse under Colonel Tempest to join with Colonel Grey at Alnwick.

Scoutmaster Major Sanderson, who had already been active in Northumberland, Durham and Yorkshire, but who had hitherto leisure enough for organising horse races and routine administration, was now galvanised into a fury of activity. Crisscrossing Yorkshire and the north east he was both a screen to, and a witness of, Lambert's move westward to shadow Langdale's army. A spy named Thomas Gooley was paid 5s for the risky job of entering the enemy quarters near Berwick, and others were paid various sums to report on border activity. Whilst Sanderson and the local Northumberland horse kept an eye first on Berwick, and then on Colonel Tempest, Lambert's main body marched west.[4]

By 16 June Lambert had gathered his diminutive army at Penrith. Langdale believed that these Northern Association forces numbered about 3,500, and given that his own army was no stronger, and daily expecting Scottish reinforcement, he did not risk serious engagement but withdrew to the friendly environs of Carlisle. In reality it is dubious whether Lambert yet had 3,000 men at Penrith, for it appears that the only troops presently available were his own and part of Lilburne's horse, and Bright's regiment of foot. Few reinforcements from the New Model had yet appeared, but Twistleton's horse were probably now with Lambert. The Lancashire militia troops were thought to be expected imminently.

A great commander would now have seized the opportunity to reward Lambert's temerity with an extremely bloody nose; but though Langdale was very good, and a respectable opponent for Lambert, he was not in that league. He wrote again to Hamilton imploring him to assist 'speedily'; he and Musgrave had fulfilled their part of the bargain, and now the Scots were expected to fulfil theirs. In the meantime every passing day increased the possibility that Lambert would be reinforced either by Cromwell, or by Lancashire Militia troops. Three days later Langdale's communication was confirmed by another, this time from Sir Philip Musgrave, emphasising that the royalist army could not hang around Carlisle for ever and that the gentry of the north of England were 'resolutely bent' to hazard their lives for the cause.[5]

By 24 June a fleeting opportunity to deal decisively with the Northern Association army had passed. Langdale and Musgrave now heard that Ashton's Lancashire militia had reached Penrith. Birch's diary records how the Lancashire militia had trudged northward from Lancaster, stoping at Kirby Lonsdale on the 19 June, and capturing Beetham house a couple of days later. The weather was appalling but the men were granted free quarter; even so it was as 'miserable time for the soldiers' as any Captain Birch had seen. In two days they then advanced from Kendal, via Shap, to Penrith. Harrison's regiment had also appeared from the south to make a welcome addition to the army. Emboldened, Lambert had launched a minor raid on Rose Castle, a mere five miles from Carlisle, and captured the small royalist garrison. Lambert could now boast nearly 5,000 men though some of his units were either tired or under strength.[6]

Very probably it would now be Lambert's plan to dominate the countryside around Carlisle, and in doing so cut off supplies, especially of forage for the cavalry. Again the English royalist leaders 'humbly' begged Hamilton to make haste. Royalist opinion, realistically, was that 'England will be lost unless the Scots army presently come in'. Turner, not very reasonably, blamed Musgrave and Langdale for their own predicament, stating that although they were both of 'untainted loyaltie and gallantrie' they had 'unseasonablie' jumped the gun, giving parliament the 'pretext' to send Lambert 'with a more considerable power', a 'strong part' of the 'English' army, to stop them. It was a measure of just how far the Scottish command was out of touch with the knife edge situation.[7]

On 1 July Colonel Tempest's little expeditionary force of 500 cavalry came to grief near Morpeth, harried and mauled by Major Sanderson of Lilburne's regiment, and the Northumberland militia. Most were captured although Tempest himself made good his escape. Royalist Charles Brandling explained the loss to the Earl of Lannark by letter and 'not without blushing', as a result of faulty intelligence. Sanderson recorded simply in his diary that 50 'grand officers' and 400 troopers were taken and escorted by him to Newcastle. Lambert wrote to parliament on 2, 4 and 8 July in order to keep them appraised of events. Despite success in small skirmishes around Carlisle, including an ambush carried out by Major Haynes of Twisleton's regiment, he had been forced to detach Harrison's regiment and others to support the position in Northumberland.[8]

Elsewhere in the kingdom parliamentarian fortunes were beginning to revive. In Kent royalist resistance had already been smashed by Lord General Fairfax at the battle of Maidstone, and in the south east it was only Essex, Colchester and rebel ships from the fleet which now posed a threat. In south Wales Cromwell was now making progress against Pembroke, so much so that parliament was asking that he send whatever troops could be spared to the north. As each regiment became available it was sent to join Lambert. During July half the New Model would find itself strung out along the roads of south

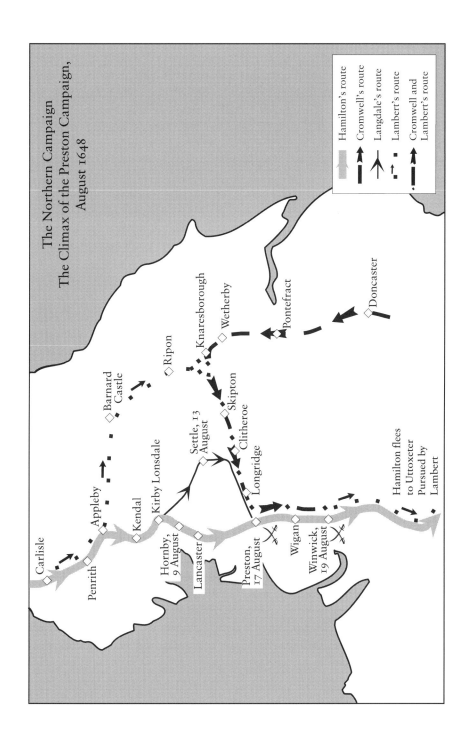

The Northern Campaign
The Climax of the Preston Campaign,
August 1648

Hamilton's route
Cromwell's route
Langdale's route
Lambert's route
Cromwell and
Lambert's route

Carlisle
Penrith
Appleby
Barnard Castle
Kendal
Kirby Lonsdale
Ripon
Knaresborough
Wetherby
Pontefract
Doncaster
Settle, 13 August
Skipton
Clitheroe
Longridge
Hornby, 9 August
Lancaster
Preston, 17 August
Wigan
Winwick, 19 August
Hamilton flees to Uttoxeter
Pursued by Lambert

Wales, the midlands and the north. The long marches, first from the south
east to south Wales, and then from here to Preston, were signal feats of arms
and endurance, but they were also a high risk strategy. Had Langdale defeated
Lambert, or Hamilton invaded quickly parliamentarian England's last bastion
would have been caught spread over the countryside in penny packets.

At this juncture Hamilton actually wrote to Lambert from Annan, appealing
for him to desert the cause of parliament and join him. The way he outlined
the Scottish cause to his antagonist was revealing; according to him the objectives of the Scottish parliament were to free the king from 'base
imprisonment', settle the question of religion, free the English parliament from
the restraints under which it laboured, and deal with the threat of the 'great
forces' drawn up on the Scottish border. Whilst some of this appeared perfectly
reasonable, the last point was both disingenuous and threatening, indeed it
could be read as a pretext for invasion. If Hamilton ever sincerely believed
that Lambert would desert his cause he was swiftly disabused by the reply,
penned on 8 July. In his response Lambert pointed out that he had been 'most
tender' to avoid giving any offence to 'our brethren of Scotland', and that his
objective in arms was simply to deal with the rebellious Sir Marmaduke
Langdale and his 'papist' friends. What was more the English parliament was
free, and as a result of the trust it gave him, he was bound 'to the utmost' of
his power to oppose all forces, 'raised or brought into this kingdom', without
the authority of parliament.

Finally it happened. On the same day Lambert wrote his reply the first
contingent of the Scottish army, which had been gathered at Annan over the
past two weeks, crossed the border: with a strength of 9,000 to 10,000 this
body proceeded in stately fashion to relieve the pressure on Carlisle. The
Scottish progress was reported by the local militia units of Colonels Benson
and Briggs from Kendal and Barrow who lacked the resources for any serious
intervention. Langdale was already pushing forward against Lambert, and the
Northern Association and their Lancashire allies had no option but to fall
back: Lambert was now outnumbered by about 13,000 to 5,000. Still the rain
continued, and as Samuel Birch put it 'such a wet time this time of year hath
not beene seene in memory of man'. On 14 July there was a skirmish at
Penrith; Lambert did well to extricate his army and fall back again, this time
to Appleby.

Again the enemy came up, and on the 17th Lambert's army had its closest
call. Scottish cavalry caught some of the Lancashire militia unprotected. As
Captain Birch recalled,

> The Scots fell upon us before we were aware, our horse being – the greatest
> part – absent; drave up our horse guards within our centryes and quarters
> of foote, drew out partyes which kept them off from us till night, and made

divers works, but by day breake in the morning wee march't away. I had the reareguard of the foote with major Greenlishe.[9]

They got off very lightly with only four or five killed and a few others wounded. According to Lambert's report Captain Henry Cromwell's lieutenant was killed and Lieutenant Sheeres was taken prisoner, but the most famous casualty of the skirmish was New Model Colonel Thomas Harrison. He had charged into the enemy with the few available horse, but ' being more forward and bold, then his men did second him', was soon in trouble. He grabbed at an enemy flag, but was worsted by the swords of his antagonists, badly cut across a wrist, and slightly pricked in the back and thigh. He survived, but it was enough to put him out of action for the remainder of the campaign. There were other losses however because the weather and the hard marching was beginning to take its toll. In Birch's company alone there had now been three desertions and one taken sick.

Following the fight Lambert again retreated, this time to Barnard Castle, keeping himself between the enemy and his Yorkshire powerbase. Even Lambert realised that this unequal war could not go on for ever and he wrote to parliament again, with concern if not desperation, requesting 'speedy supply', lest there be dire consequences for the kingdom. Hamilton did not immediately press his advantage, and instead waited at Kirby Thore for the rest of the Scottish army to join him. Units were still trickling up to the main army to swell Hamilton's number to about 15,000 or so, not counting Callander's regiment who became the new garrison of Carlisle. At Kendal Hamilton met Munro, who had ridden on ahead of his 'New Scots' army to confer with him. Hamilton could have waited longer again, but it was apparent that Munro regarded his men as an allied force, rather than an integral part of the Scottish army. At last, and perhaps finally sensing that time did matter, Hamilton set off, leaving Munro to proceed with Tyldesley and Musgrave.

Lambert had won no battle, but with a tiny force had slowed the progress of a huge army to a snail's pace. Hamilton's next push came on 26 July but the odds in his favour were already beginning to shorten, for by now more New Model reinforcements were trickling in to aid Lambert. Fairfax's foot had joined the beleaguered Northern Association and Lancashire forces from the south east in early July. Cromwell now felt he could do without six troops of horse, and had accordingly dispatched three troops of Colonel Scroope's and two of dragoons to Lambert and a further troop of horse to Cheshire. The parliamentarians took up a good defensive position near Brough, blocking a pass through the hills at Stainmore. Again the Scottish royalist army obtained a minor tactical victory and the parliamentarians were forced from their position, but again Lambert was not conclusively defeated.[10]

Ominously rumour was reaching the parliamentarian camp of dissensions between the Scots and their allies; in the view of some of Langdale's men it was always the English who were put 'on the hardest duty'. Neither were the Scots endearing themselves to the local populations. According to one victim they were a plague of locusts who 'left nothing portable' in their wake. Another said extortion was their speciality, kidnapping the sons and daughters of the gentry against payments and supplies. Rape was also said to be taking place, with some women forced 'before their friends' faces'. From York came the exasperated opinion that it was only southerner's ignorance of Scottish depredations which allowed them to hold a better regard of the Scots than those who actually have to live near them.

Pembroke castle had finally surrendered on 11 July and a week later Cromwell was himself on the road with a substantial body of reinforcements, which appear to have totalled at least three foot regiments, one horse regiment and some dragoons. Parliament then believed that his force totalled 1,200 horse and 3,000 foot at maximum. Long as the march ahead was, Cromwell did not intend to sacrifice strategic considerations purely for speed. The shortest route would probably have been across Wales, but the terrain and lack of supplies would have enervated his army before it reached the English border. A sensible alternative would have been to head east, up through the Welsh marches, via Shrewsbury and thence to Chester or Stockport. Very probably this is the route that most commanders would have chosen, and indeed the units which had already been released were sent by this route.[11]

Cromwell went one better, going as far east as Leicester. It was a very long way, but it had the advantage that it placed his little army in the dead centre of the country, between his enemies and London. This would allow him considerable scope for manoeuvre, and the chances of the Scots getting past without a fight were negligible. It showed either supreme confidence in Lambert's ability, or extreme indifference to his fate, for the time delay could easily have led to Lambert, who now faced about 20,000 with about a quarter of that number, being crushed. Thus it was that Cromwell's march took him via Gloucester and Warwick. His troops remained disciplined although they were not without hardship, as one explained in the *Moderate Intelligencer*:

> Our Marches [are] long, and want of shoes and stockings gives discouragement to our soldiers, having received no pay these many months to buy them, nor can any procure unless we plunder, which was never heard of by any under the Lieutenant General's conduct nor will be, though they march barefoot, which many have done, since our advance from Wales.

On 1 August Cromwell had reached Leicester. His grateful troops now received 2,500 pairs of shoes, provided by the manufactory at Northampton. Prisoners who had accompanied him from Wales were sent to Nottingham.

Cromwell was also offered the services of an extra troop of horse from Herefordshire, under Captain Dolphin, but whether these actually fought at Preston is unrecorded. Hurrying on, the New Model now headed for Doncaster, which he reached a week after Leicester. Here his ammunition was replenished, fresh supply having been brought from Hull: some authorities also suggest that he recruited his regiments back up to strength.[12]

Lambert's command, though sodden, and slightly battered from several rough handlings, remained unbroken and was again falling back via Ripon and Knaresborough. On 12 August, between Knaresborough and Wetherby, victory became a remote possibility, for there Cromwell met Lambert and parliament's meagre forces were for the first time concentrated in one spot. Between them the New Model, Northern Association, and Lancashire forces now numbered about 10,000 men. To have allowed Lambert to escape and join with Cromwell was serious, but it was something which could have happened to anyone faced with an opposition of such calibre. To remain ignorant of the fact as long as Hamilton did was a serious personal failing. Despite Cromwell's success in joining with Lambert the parliamentarian forces were still outnumbered slightly more than two to one. To an average or good general their course of action would be obvious: they would find a good defensive position athwart Hamilton's road south and force him to attack them, at a disadvantage, on ground of their choosing, before he could either threaten London or join up with royalists in the south. It is a measure of Cromwell's confidence in his maker and himself that he chose to do otherwise.

In the meantime Hamilton's august procession moved slowly south. There was a lengthy stop at Kendal, and if Turner is to be believed the Scottish army had reached Hornby in Lancashire before any final decision as to the route had been taken. According to his version of events Baillie was in favour of going through Lancashire, whilst Middleton and himself were for heading through Yorkshire and taking the most direct path to London. Callander, he believed, was indifferent. Turner stated that he thought that the hedges and ditches and waterlogged ground of Lancashire would make heavy going, whilst the more open country of Yorkshire was better for the cavalry. Bishop Burnet later gave a rather different version of events; in this he said that Hamilton, Baillie and Turner were all for Yorkshire, whilst it was Langdale and Callander who argued for Lancashire. Which is the correct version may never be resolved, but Turner's account is on the face of it more logical if only because he has the commander of the cavalry opting for the open cavalry country, and the commander of the infantry choosing the more cramped path.

In any event it was the Lancashire route which was selected, perhaps because it was felt that a projected rising in North Wales would lend support. Langdale was to take the van, and cover the main advance on its south and east. No further time would be wasted on Lancaster which would be besieged by Sir Thomas Tyldesley. The Scottish army would proceed down the main road, followed at a distance by Munro's 'New Scots'; they would cross the Ribble at the only available bridge in the area, at Preston, and follow what is now the 'A6' southwards. The Scottish order of march put the main body of the cavalry under Middleton out in front, and the infantry, under Baillie, following. Burnet has it that the cavalry were complaining of 'scarcity of forage in these parts' and sought permission to ride further ahead, something to which Hamilton reluctantly agreed.[13]

Cromwell's daring decision was not to fall back, but to advance rapidly and take on the enemy. Accordingly the parliamentarians advanced to Otley on 13 August. Langdale who was at Settle that day, appears to have heard rumours that the enemy was marching in his direction, but as yet there was no firm evidence. He later met Callander and other Scottish officers near Clitheroe: 'but for the present the intelligence was, that the parliament forces were divided, some part whereof were marched to Colne, and so to Manchester, to relieve that town in case we should presse upon it.'[14]

No urgent action was therefore taken. On the 14 Cromwell 'marching very sore', reached Skipton, and scouts probed forward into the Ribble valley. It was clear he meant business, 'casting off' his supply train and sending it to Knaresborough, ' because of the difficulty of marching therewith through Craven, and to the end we might with more expedition attend the enemy's motion'. That night Lilburne's and Twistleton's regiments of horse screened their comrades, by placing piquets and camping further forward at Gargrave. Langdale said later that he now had intelligence that the enemy scouts were no more than three miles away; he communicated the facts as he knew them to Hamilton, and began to move his command west to join up with the Scots. Whether Langdale's early warnings were as explicit as he made out is open to question, since Turner specifically denies it; nevertheless Langdale was alert enough to put his army in a defensive posture.[15]

Further evidence of the seriousness of the position soon came. On the 15 Cromwell himself was at Gisburn, a mere ten miles from Clitheroe. That night his advanced patrols captured the hapless Colonel Tempest, a captain and 14 men – two royalist officers and four troopers were killed. Hamilton should by now have been taking vigorous countermeasures, calling in his cavalry, seeking information from patrols, issuing urgent demands that Munro should force march to their assistance, and selecting a place to fight if needs be. That he did not requires explanation. The traditional answers to the Duke's inactivity have been Turner's statement that he simply did not know, and the less charitable reasons of bad generalship and complete willingness to sacrifice Langdale whilst the Scots proceeded on their way.

Another, and equally likely conclusion, is that both he and Callander did hear an approximation of the true position from Langdale's messengers on the 15 and 16, but refused to believe them. After all it was hardly likely that Cromwell would march from the south east to south Wales, to the midlands, then to Yorkshire, and, hardly pausing for breath, march another 50 miles and fall immediately on an enemy twice his size. In short such impertinence and impetuosity was hardly credible; it appeared much more likely that the skirmishing in the Ribble valley was another tip and run from the troublesome Lambert, or a foolhardy effort by Ashton's Lancashire militia to delay them. Thus it was that Munro remained north of Lancaster; Middleton and the bulk of the Scottish cavalry continued to forage south of the Ribble with general orders to proceed to Wigan; and that Baillie's infantry, with the artillery limbered and only a small rearguard of horse, were north of the river in a lengthy column of march on their way to Preston.

On 16 August Cromwell held a council of war with his senior officers at Hodder bridge, near Clitheroe. According to him the main issue discussed was whether to proceed south, via Whalley and 'interpose between the enemy and his further progress into Lancashire and so southward', or to go north of the Ribble in the direction of Preston and immediately engage the enemy, who

The Hodder bridge over the river Ribble, scene of the council of war which sealed parliamentary strategy the day before the battle. The river itself was perhaps the most vital topographic feature of the campaign.

would stand his ground to allow Munro to join him. It was a similar dilemma to those which Cromwell had already rehearsed at Knaresborough and Leicester, and very probably he had already made up his mind. The common soldiery were not consulted but had they been they might well have chosen to get the whole thing over and done with as soon as possible. By now there were many in the parliamentarian ranks who were on their second or third set of footwear, who had marched more than 500 miles carrying a knapsack and trailing a pike, had fought a siege, and been rained on for weeks solid. As Cromwell summed it up:

> It was thought that to engage the enemy to fight was our business; and the reason aforesaid giving us hopes that our marching on the north side of Ribble would effect it, it was resolved that we should march over the bridge; which accordingly we did; and that night quartered the whole army in a field by Stonyhurst Hall, being Mr Sherburn's house.

Stonyhurst was not then the grand school that it has since become, but the hall of a minor Catholic gentleman. On the night of 16 August 1648 Stonyhurst appeared even less imposing than usual. Lancashire Militia Captain Samuel Birch realised that the enemy had been there before them, leaving 'the quarters so bare as an enemy could'. In any event there was no place for him inside so he slept in the field with the men.[16]

5

'Bloudy Preston', 17 August 1648

URING THE NIGHT OF 16 TO 17 AUGUST, Langdale's scouts confirmed the awful truth. A sizeable body of parliamentarian troops was headed towards Preston from the north east. Still there was no reaction from the Scots; Middleton's cavalry were not recalled, and Baillie's infantry would resume their march in the morning, spread out and intent on making the river crossing. The parliamentarian forces had broken camp early and were soon bearing down through the damp morning on Langdale's army.

Cromwell had fronted his marching columns with a very strong 'forlorn hope', or body of skirmishers. The 500 mounted skirmishers were commanded by Major Smithson of Lilburne's horse, and the 200 foot by Major Pownall and Captain Hodgson, both of Bright's foot. There were also 200 of Okey's dragoons. Predictably, in view of their local knowledge, Cromwell had chosen Northern Association troops to lead the way. By Longridge Chapel, about six miles from Preston the skirmishers of both sides made contact; a running fight broke out, with neither party in formed bodies, the cavalry making short rushes, and the infantry making the best use of the limited cover available.[1]

Given the relatively open nature of the country south and west of Longridge, and that he was outnumbered nearly three to one, Langdale made the best possible decision in the circumstances. He opted for a fighting retreat in the direction of Preston, with the aim of gaining the cover of the enclosures on the north side of town. Surely by then sufficient of the Scottish forces would be available to halt the New Model.

The Preston towards which Langdale's men were retreating was very different to the modern town. Now the population is about 130,000, but in those days it was a market town, hardly touched by industry, whose population scarce exceeded 2,000 – a pittance compared to the huge bodies of troops manoeuvring about it. The main feature was a large market square, with a smaller fish market to one side: three major thoroughfares adjoined, Fishergate, Friargate and Church Street. This last was relatively open, substantial buildings petering out about the church, and the northern part of Church Street was then known as Fenkell Street. Other passages existing in 1648 included Anchor Court, Broadgate, which joined Fishergate to the ferry boat which crossed the Ribble to Penwortham, and Cheapside which was adorned with a butter cross. Two structures would perhaps have impressed the seventeenth-century traveller more than the others, the parish church and the old Guildhall. The solid church had featured in the storm of the town in 1643, when the royalists had held its tower. The Guildhall, right at the hub of the medieval town, doubled as a courthouse. Underneath it ran the 'Shambles' or two rows of butcher's shops. The castle mound at Penwortham across the river still existed, but the fortress was long since ruined.[2]

The most important geographical feature was the river. Modern commuters and frustrated town planners will be able to confirm that it dominates all north-south traffic, and at the time of the battle there was only one bridge, situated thirty or forty yards west of the current London Road bridge. This bridge could also be reached by more than one passage way, leading perpendicular from Church Street, one of which was named Stoneygate and another Cockshutts Backside, now more decorously known as Turk's Head Court. There were two other possible ways across the Ribble, short of swimming; the ford at Penwortham, the use of which was dependant on the tides, and the little ferry boat, but neither was as convenient or strategically useful as the bridge. Above the bridge in the region of Fishwick, and as far as Brockholes, the land from the plateau on which Preston was situated sloped steeply down to the meandering Ribble. At Fishwick, literally 'the place where fish is sold' a track now known as Watery Lane ran down the slope across the bottoms to the river, and a branch of the track led through the marshy ground toward the bridge. Known to locals and antiquaries, but too small to be marked on contemporary printed maps these features were to be of considerable importance on the afternoon of 17 August 1648.[3]

By late morning Langdale had been pushed back to Eaves Brook, a shallow stream in a sharply sided cut, just outside the northern enclosures of Preston. He had been retreating slowly but steadily, but now he was in a good defensive position, with his main body behind hedges on the Preston side, and his skirmishers still on the brook itself. The hour had come to stand and buy time whilst Hamilton ordered his Scots for battle. Langdale's frontage almost certainly stretched from the line now occupied by Pope lane in the east across to the fringes of Holme Slack in the west, a distance of over three quaters of a mile. His left flank, which probably terminated short of the present location of Coniston Road was therefore not securely anchored. As he had only 3,000 infantry in total it seems likely there were few reserves behind his main and skirmish lines. The precise location of one infantry regiment is known for sure: Carleton's, which was just right of centre around Ribbleton Avenue. In 1648 Ribbleton was no more than a hamlet, the main landmark being a windmill north of the brook. It is also likely that Brockholes and Boilton woods were larger than they are now.

Hitherto Cromwell's main force had been pushing down the Longridge road at the maximum pace the muddy track would allow behind his advanced guard. Meeting the solid obstruction of Langdale's main force he deployed into battle formation, Reade's, Deane's and Pride's infantry regiments to the right of the lane, Bright's and Fairfax's to the left. Thornhaugh and Twisleton's horse supported the right, whilst his own and Harrison's horse continued on down the road. Ashton's Lancashire brigade formed a second line behind his regulars. On the left, nearest to the Ribble, he put his 'remaining' cavalry; these were, by process of elimination, almost certainly Lambert's regiment of horse, three troops of Adrian Scroope's horse, and the Lancashire horse.

His formation was therefore a strong front line of about 3,500 infantry, with

Watery Lane running down the scarp to Fishwick Bottoms. By means of this narrow but well-concealed defile the Lancashire Militia would succeed in outflanking the English Royalists.

three bodies of cavalry, each almost 1,000 strong in its midst, to its left, and right, the second line infantry being considerably weaker, forming a reserve of perhaps 1,600 foot. The forlorn, or skirmish line, contained nearly ten percent of his army with 900 horse and foot. Given the numbers, and the fact that the central group of cavalry's location and formation is known, and that there would have been gaps between units, it is probable that the total frontage was over a mile. Since this was rather longer than Langdale's front his right hand units extended beyond Langdale's left, on the ground now occupied by Coniston road. Leaving his own and Harrison's horse on the main road was the least conventional part of the deployment, but a good deal of the ground was, as Cromwell described it, 'totally inconvenient' for the horse 'being all enclosure and miry ground'. He may therefore have felt that his crack regiments were best off on the lane, where, although they were on a very narrow frontage, they were unimpeded by hedges across their front and would add weight to the centre.

There remains to this day a little hummock off the new Eastway, near Sherwood, which is marked on maps as 'Cromwell's Mound'. It is now isolated by the road and new industrial development, but a third of a millennium ago it may have furnished 'old Noll' his first vantage point to view the field as his troops marched down and deployed across the land where Fulwood now lies. If so Cromwell had moved, at least temporarily, out to the rear of the right flank of his army. Here several points would have been of interest: doubtless he would have attempted to ascertain how far the royalist line might extend, but equally he may have been attempting to determine whether indeed the Scots lay to his right flank. Langdale's hope, that Hamilton would appear and fall on the parliamentarian right, was Cromwell's fear.

Meanwhile, to the front, skirmishing was already in its third or fourth hour, and although there were probably only a handful of casualties so far, the 'forlorn hopes' of both sides were nearing exhaustion. Pownall and Hodgson drew up short of the brook and waited for their straggling companies to catch up. At that moment the general appeared and commanded them to march.

> We not having half our men come up desired a little patience; he gives out the word, March ! and so we drew over a little common, where our horse was drawn up, and came to a ditch, and the enemy let fly at us (a company of Langdale's men that was newly raised). They shot at the skies, which did so encourage our men that they were willing to venture upon any attempt.

Hodgson advanced, jumped the ditch, and looked around. To his surprise, on the left, in the direction of what is now Ribbleton Avenue, he discovered that he had outflanked a party of the enemy who were waiting in ambush behind a hedge for Smithson's horse. These were a company of Carleton's regiment,

Assheton Place, pictured in 1996: one of many similar streets on the boundaries of Fulwood and Ribbleton named in commemoration of the commanders of the 1648 campaign, and indeed occupying a small part of the field. Cromwell Road is perhaps the best known thoroughfare, but fittingly enough others nearby are named after Lambert, Carleton, Munro and Hamilton.

which, finding the enemy behind it, beat a hasty retreat towards their main body. Hodgson charged after their leader, but this man, later discovered to be Carleton himself, made good his escape.[4]

Now Langdale's infantry launched a well-timed counter attack, as Hodgson described it:

> The enemy coming against us with a great body of colours, we had no way to shelter ourselves but drew over a lane where Major Smithson was, and there we kept them in play so long as our ammunition lasted, and still kept our ground.
>
> At last comes a party of Scots lanciers, and charged Major Smithson in the lane, passing by us, and put him to retreat, but they were routed immediately, and one of their commanders was running away, and I being aware of him stepped into the lane, and dismounted him, and clapped into the saddle, and our horse came up in pursuit.

Cromwell's Mound, located in a field between the aptly named Oliver's Place, the Eastway and Durton Lane, and skirted by the trickle of Moss Leach Brook. Though now overshadowed by a modern stationery warehouse, there is ample evidence nearby of hedgerows of some antiquity. Cromwell's use of the mound as an observation point is difficult to prove, though scouting around here would have been a sensible precaution to ensure the security of the right flank of the army.

Even as Cromwell's and Harrison's regiments of 'Ironsides' were clearing the lane (now Ribbleton Avenue), critical decisions were being made little more than a mile away.

By noon, according to Bishop Burnet, the main bodies of the Scottish infantry were drawing up on Preston Moor; the areas now known as Sharoe Green, and the western side of Moor Park, along Garstang Road. If Langdale had his way these would have marched quickly on Ribbleton 'to have flanked the enemy' – but despite Sir Lewis Dyves' prompting it was not to be. Hamilton rode ahead towards the Ribble bridge to 'view the field for a convenient leaguer'. The battle on his left can now have been no more than a mile away, but he seemed determined to regard it as no more than a distraction, even though it must by now have been audible. At most he was prepared to feed in the rearguard of cavalry to bolster Langdale. In Hamilton's absence from the main body the Earl of Callander ordered Baillie and the infantry on towards the bridge. Now the Scottish command was in confusion.

Looking westwards along Eaves Brook, from a point within a few yards of the end of Fairfax Road. Around this area was the fierce skirmish fight in which Captain Hodgson and his colleagues eventually succeeded in securing the line of the stream.

The general returning, and thinking to have found the foot still on the moor, met Baylie on the bridge, who told him he had received orders from Callander to draw over the whole body of foot; but hearing that Langdale was hotly engaged with the enemy he halted there, till he saw what the event of the action might be: which the general approved.[5]

Callander now rode up and an argument ensued. Callander wanted to know why the march had been stopped, and why Hamilton could possibly want to keep his foot (on the bridge) and his horse (still near Wigan) so far apart. Hamilton informed him that Baillie was only following his orders, but he bowed so far as to direct the infantry to cross the bridge to the Walton-le-Dale side and take position. Returning to Preston Moor Hamilton and Callander found the rearguard of the army, some horse and two brigades of foot. Even as they did so it must have been horribly apparent that a blunder had been made; firing from Ribbleton was now reaching a crescendo, and intelligence from a few parliamentarian prisoners made it clear that Langdale had been

right all along. The enemy attacking from the direction of Longridge was no
spoiling a force, but Cromwell with the main army.

According to Edward Robinson, the probable author of the *Discourse of
the Warr in Lancashire*, the Scots wilfully neglected Langdale, and Hamilton's
reaction to his urgent requests for support had been to remark 'Let them alone
– the English dogs are but killing one another'. The Scots accounts do perhaps
ring truer in this particular, and what they reveal is poor intelligence combined
with indecision, if not incompetence. Hamilton now sent 700 foot to Langdale's
aid, which may or may not have arrived, plus the lancers that Hodgson saw,
but it was too little too late. The New Model was now pushing the English
royalists back, hedge by hedge towards Preston. In the words of one description,
Cromwell

> set upon them very fearsly beating them up all the way to Preston . . . many
> were killed, some being trodden into the dirt in the lanes with the horses
> feet, the wayes were so deep. Abundance were killed in the fields on the
> east syd of Preston and so did drive them doune toward Ribble bridge.[6]

Deepdale and Fishwick were built up in the Victorian era making it
difficult to picture the fierce struggle, but we do at least know where some of
the hedges and field boundaries they fought over lay. Kuerden's map of the
1680s shows shrubs and small trees along the sides of Ribbleton Lane, and we
know that Acregate lane existed at that time, almost certainly lined with a
hedge.[7]

It was now well into the afternoon, perhaps after two, and Langdale was
hard pressed indeed. He had succeeded in halting the enemy skirmishers, and
temporarily checking the cavalry. Now Cromwell was bringing up the well-
ordered bodies of the infantry to the hedge lines, with Fairfaxes and Bright's
carrying the bulk of the struggle. What Langdale probably could not see from
his position, somewhere between the present Skeffington Road and Acregate,
was that there were odd movements beginning to happen in the second rank
of the parliamentarian army. Ashton's Lancashire militia regiments had begun
to wheel left, and disappear company at a time, down the steep slope of the
valley towards Fishwick bottoms. According to Hodgson's recollection the
manoeuvre was instigated by Lambert, who had been fighting on foot alongside
Colonel Bright and his men. Lambert spotted Hodgson on his captured horse
and

> He ordered me to fetch up the Lancashire regiment; and God brought me
> off, both horse and myself. The bullets flew freely; then was the heat of
> battle that day. I came down to the muir, where I met with Major Jackson,
> that belonged to Ashton's regiment, and about three hundred men came up;
> and I ordered him to march, but he said he would not, till his men were

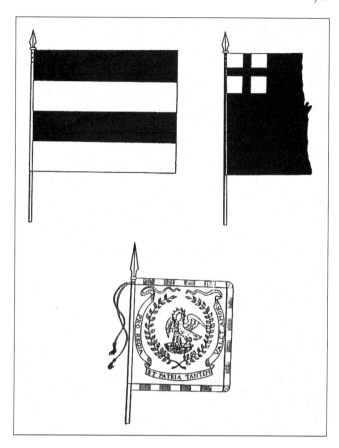

Top, two tattered English royalist colours taken during the battle, both red and white, from unidentified regiments; bottom a cornet from Tyldesley's cavalry regiment with gold pelican and wreath on a red field.

come up. A sergeant belonging to them, asked me, where should they march? I showed him the party he was to fight and like a true Englishman, marched.[8]

However the orders were relayed, and whether the selector of the route was Ashton, Lambert or the humble Captain Hodgson, the Lancashire troops began to pass in small units, down the narrow defile of Watery Lane. Even today, after building and drainage work, the lane is still 'watery', with a small stream emerging from the track. One of the companies going this way was that of Samuel Birch; at some point Birch's regiment was reorganised, so that assault groups were formed, one of pikes and one of muskets, to lead the attack on the Ribble bridge. Birch was then given command of this 'forlorn'; his ensign was to lead the pikes, his lieutenant the musketeers.

Even before the climatic struggle for the bridge had begun Thornhaugh and Twisleton's regiments of horse on the right of the parliamentarian army had become engaged with the Scottish rearguard of cavalry. Given the positions of the infantry this can only reasonably have been on the space now occupied by the built up area from Fulwood Barracks to Preston North End. According to parliamentarian J. Walton this action was quite short:

> For the Scottish horse had stood to it a charge or two, and finding such hot service, began to retreat, our horse followed them, and with their shot so galled them, that they forced them to run, our forces persued them as farre as they could and not be endangered by the Scottish foot. Then our horse retreated in very good time to relieve our left wing.[9]

Thus were the Scots left virtually bereft of cavalry, and the balance began to swing away from numbers towards the better-poised and organised enemy.

On the east things were still in the balance with Langdale still

A northern Royalist ensign.

hanging on grimly and putting up what Cromwell admitted was 'a very stiff and sturdy resistance'. In this phase of the fighting he singled out Bright's, Fairfaxes, Reade's and Ashton's Lancashire troops for particular praise: 'They often coming to push of pike and to close firing, and always making the enemy recoil'.[10]

As Langdale was pushed slowly back his force edged a little to the right, perhaps because he now realised he was being outflanked by Ashton, or maybe his troops simply wished to secure their line of retreat across the Ribble. As a parliamentarian report in the *Moderate Intelligencer* described it:

> The battle on a sodain waxed very hot, and there was a furious dispute for the space of two hours or there abouts. They had so thick lined the hedges and lanes, that they galled both our horse and foot, at length our men forced them to give back, but yet the contention was very long and much ado we had to get ground upon them, till our regiments of foot came up and flank't them.

With Deane's and Pride's infantry beginning to press on the royalist left and

The view south over the Ribble flood plain at Fishwick Bottoms: even after drainage work the valley floor is still inundated in bad weather. The Lancashire Militia under Ashton made their way down the slope through the trees on the right of the picture; the recently renovated buildings in the centre are those of Fishwick Hall Farm.

Ashton working around their right, it was now only a matter of time, either before Langdale's command collapsed, or the Scots came to their aid in serious numbers. Hamilton did not change course, and after what Cromwell estimated as a four hour fight the English royalist regiments began to collapse in disorder with many slain and others taken prisoner. The first four troops of Cromwell's cavalry regiment broke through the remnants of Langdale's command and thundered down Church Street, clearing it.

It was now late in the afternoon, perhaps approaching five o'clock, and most of the Scots had crossed the Ribble bridge, but some were still trapped to the north; including two brigades of infantry, a few of the cavalry rearguard and Hamilton himself. Munro was still many miles away, so Hamilton made for the Penwortham ford accompanied by his Lifeguard. According to Turner Hamilton's party found the ford impassable and were now harried by parliamentarian cavalry.

> The Duke fac'd about, and put tuo troops of them to retreate; but so soon as we turned from them, they turned upon us. The Duke facing the second time, charged them which succeeded well. Being pursued a third time, my Lord Duke cryd to charge once more for King Charles. One trooper refusing,

he beate him with his sword. At that charge we put the enemie so fare
behind us, that he could not overtake us.[11]

Hamilton and his entourage now swam the river, showing, in Turner's
opinion, 'as much personall valour as any man could be capable of'. At some
point Marmaduke Langdale extricated himself from the debacle of Deepdale
and Fishwick and joined the Duke's party. The infantry left on the Preston
side were defeated in detail whilst the remaining Scottish cavalry on the north
side of the river for the most part made good their escape up Garstang Road,
perhaps in hopes of reaching Munro.

In the meantime Callander had managed to rejoin Baillie south of the Ribble
bridge, and had organised the defence of the crossing and its immediate
environs with 600 musketeers, whilst the main battalions of the Scottish infantry headed for Walton Hill where they would form up in a defensive posture.
Despite the protection of the river and the strength of the Scottish foot the
bridge position was exposed, being lower than the ground now occupied by
Fairfax's and Bright's infantry. As Burnet's narrative relates 'the enemy's side
was all a descent to the bridge, that was full of hedges, from which their
firemen (musketeers) played incessantly'.[12]

To make matters worse the Lancashire regiments were now attacking the
bridge from the east, having emerged in strength from the then undrained mire
of Fishwick Bottoms. A 'very hot' dispute now took place with the Lancastrians
forcing the Scots from the bridge at point of pike. Fairfax's regiment aided
them by giving covering fire from a different direction. Captain Birch was in
the thick of it, and his ensign Adam Sydall actually led the charge against the
bridge. At first the Scots replied spiritedly, and according to Birch many of
his men, including all the officers, were wounded. Miraculously none were
killed outright but it is more than probable that some would later have died
of wounds. Amongst the Scots casualties was Claude Hamilton, lieutenant
colonel to the Duke of Hamilton's own regiment, his arm broken by a musket
ball. The Duke himself was beginning to realise that the position was untenable,
but even before he could do anything about it the bridge was taken, and the
enemy swarmed across, killing many and seizing the few buildings south of
the bridge. Some such, much like those noted by Cromwell in 1648, appear
on the map of the 1680s.[13]

Now came a lull. Both the victor and the vanquished were feeling the effects
of a day long struggle. Added to this the battle front was now very narrow
and although Cromwell's men had managed to get a toe hold across the Ribble,
and were even now securing another smaller bridge across the Darwen, there
was now no way, short of an uphill frontal assault, that they would make
further headway. As Milton elegantly put it the 'Darwen stream' was 'with
the blood of Scots embued'; but although the parliamentarians had won a

Charles Cattermole's famous painting of the Battle of Preston. The episode represented is the attack on Walton Bridge, though time and space appear to have been telescoped somewhat. (*Harris Museum, Preston*)

significant success the Scots still had a threatening force in being, as big as, or larger than Cromwell's.[14]

Nonetheless there was confidence that the enemy had been dealt a serious blow. Tradition has it that Cromwell spent the remainder of the night in a house south of the Ribble bridge, one subsequently used as a public house and restaurant. But his dispatches that night were noted as written at 'Preston', and given the uncertain nature of the hold south of the river it is equally possible he stayed in the town. Even so there were now thousands of parliamentarian troops in and around Preston and Walton-le-Dale; few buildings can therefore have been unvisited by the soldiery. Whatever the case it was now Cromwell's main concern to inform the Lancashire Committee at Manchester of the situation. In a hasty letter, which was also later relayed to London, he described the enemy as 'broken' with 'nothing hindering the ruin of that part of the enemy's army but the night'. It was vital that he encourage the people of Manchester to resist, should the Scots army, or any part of it, come in their direction.

In truth it was still possible that the Scots might escape, or worse that they would effect a juncture with the cavalry under Middleton, or even with Munro. With some of his cavalry pursuing the Scottish rearguard north towards Lancaster, and scattering others west into the Fylde, he considered his main objective to be to prevent the Scots getting past him, either by fording the

Ribble at Preston or marching via Whalley. To this end Cromwell sent off
seven troops of horse to hinder any march towards Whalley.[15]

Far from making an aggressive move on Whalley the Scottish command was
actually in a defensive, even depressive, frame of mind. With his soldiers
building flimsy bivouacs on Walton Hill Hamilton called his senior officers
together and examined his options. According to Turner there were really only
two: to wait on Walton Hill for Middleton and the cavalry, who had been
summoned to join them; or else to march away under cover of darkness and
meet up with him on the way. Most favoured escape, though Baillie and Turner
apparently pressed him to hold his ground; in retrospect this latter plan may
have been the best course of action. However as Turner relates,

> all the arguments were used, as the impossibilitie of a safe retreat from ane
> enemie so powerful of horse, in foule weather, and extremelie deepe way,
> our sojors exceeding wet, wearie, and hungrie, the inevitable loss of all our
> ammunition, [but] could not move my lord Duke by his authoritie to
> contradict the shameful resolution taken by the major part of his of-
> ficers'.[16]

The decision was therefore for a 'drumless march', and to steal away into the
night. To have shifted the guns, baggage and ammunition from their exposed
position on the hill would have made the move obvious. Hamilton therefore
ordered that it all be destroyed, after the main force had departed. Whether
bad weather foiled this attempted arson, or whether the soldiers detailed to
the work thought more of their own safety is not recorded, but these significant
prizes would soon fall into Cromwell's hands. At least the Scottish march was
not immediately discovered and the army set off dejectedly towards Wigan,
with little cavalry, no artillery and no supply wagons.

6

Last Stand

N THE SPACE BETWEEN THE TWO ARMIES parliamentarian cavalry searched and probed in the dark. Captain Hodgson has it that a Captain Pockley with a mere six or eight horsemen 'kept a gap-stead of their whole army'. More interesting to the remainder of the patrolling cavalry was Hamilton's baggage, which, according to one eye-witness 'strewed' the way, along with arms and provisions. On the hill above Walton-le-Dale troopers found the bulk of the Scottish 'train', including all the 'Duke's artillery and cariages'; they turned the wagons around and began to lead them back in the direction of Preston. As they did so they 'threw over that wherein was all his plate, as they brought it down the hill'. According to another account the Scots had also thrown together some bivouacs, or 'cab-bins', on the hill. These would also have been a prime target for looting. By the small bridge over the Darwen a house began to burn, set alight, the parliamentarians thought, as a further impediment to pursuit.[1]

Cromwell, whom we last located in Preston sometime before midnight dictating his dispatch to Manchester, was not inactive long. Popular mythology has it that he also spent a night at Astley Hall, Chorley, but given the whirlwind pace of events he cannot have stopped for much time anywhere. As soon as it was realised that the Scots had fled concealed by the dark and foul weather, Cromwell was again urging his army on, yet in his own words 'we were so wearied with the dispute that we did not so well attend the enemy's going off as might have been'. He marched on with about 6,000 men leaving Colonel Ashton in Preston. In the event the Scots made about three miles before the roundheads were again snapping at their heels. Colonel Thornhaugh was ordered to lead the New Model's advanced guard of horse with directions to make the enemy stand, if he could, until the rest of the army could close up.

General Middleton, leading the bulk of the Scottish cavalry, was by now appraised of the situation, and had led his men back to join up with Hamilton. Riding via Chorley he narrowly missed his commander's main body which was now heading south on the Standish road. Meeting the advancing par-liamentarians Middleton would now do his best to screen the retreat.

Thornhaugh, harrying the Scots hard with about 2,500 horse and dragoons, was at last confronted by a determined body of Scottish lancers at Chorley. Leading his men in person, he pressed on too boldly and, not wearing any armour, 'was slain, being run into the body thigh and head by the Enemy's lancers'. For such conduct Cromwell was to describe him as a man as 'faithful and gallant' in the service of parliament as any. Despite such mishaps the fortunes of Hamilton's still sizable but beleaguered force were now going from bad to worse.[2]

The pressure was kept up relentlessly, with most of the army now on the move. Captain Samuel Birch recorded that the local Lancashire troops were left in Preston to guard about 3,000 prisoners and to watch against any threats, either from Monroe or Sir Thomas Tyldesley. Also in the keeping of the Lancashire Militia and now being counted, were vast quantities of captured baggage and munitions; these already included £5,000 worth of goods, 4,000 firearms, 20 pieces of ordnance, eight barrels of gunpowder and four carts of ammunition. One of the more unusual prizes seized was at least one cart load of blue bonnets, the headgear which gave the Scottish troops their nickname 'blue caps'. More plunder would soon follow.[3]

All through 18 August, the marching, chasing and skirmishing continued. As Cromwell stated in his letter to parliament,

> Our horse still prosecuted the Enemy; killing and taking divers all the way. At last the enemy drew up within three miles of Wigan; and by that time our army was come up, they drew off again, and recovered Wigan before we could attempt any thing upon them. We lay that night in the field close by the enemy; being very dirty and weary, and having marched twelve miles of such ground as I never rode in all my life, the day being very wet. We had some skirmishing, that night with the enemy, near the town; where we took General Van Druske and a Colonel, and killed some principal officers, and took about a hundred prisoners.[4]

The night of the 18th was strange in many ways. Both armies were too exhausted and disorganised to fight a set piece battle, yet during the welcome hours of moonlit darkness there were deeds of both shame and chivalry. A small fight took place on Standish Moor. Sir James Turner, following in the wake of Hamilton and Callander, was with the last of the Scottish infantry into Wigan; here he witnessed one of the worst moments of panic. He halted his pikemen in an attempt to stay some routing cavalry, who refused to halt. To save bloodshed he then tried to order the infantry out of the way; the pikemen interpreted this as treachery and at least one attempted to run his senior officer through. Turner was wounded in the thigh, which made him 'forget all rules of modestie, prudence and discretion' and the horse now came helterskelter 'not through', but over, their own foot. The 'great and poor' town of Wigan was also thoroughly plundered by the hungry Scots. In the midst of the misery Hamilton remembered his wounded brother Colonel Claud Hamilton who had been captured, and he penned a note to the enemy general pleading for his 'civil usage'. Other losses included Colonel Urry, shot in the head and then captured, Colonel Innes, captured, and Colonel Lockheart trampled by routing horse.[4]

Turner, who had been without sleep and food for two nights, slumped into a chair to rest, but the 'constant alarums' of the enemy were so disturbing that he had no choice but to remount and join the column. Notwithstanding his wound he fell asleep in the saddle. Behind him spo-

New Model trooper.

radic skirmishing continued and stragglers were overrun and killed by the pursuers. Hodgson, with the pursuit, recalled 'pitching upon a muir' outside Wigan 'towards morning'. Here he enjoyed a 'pint of strong waters' with his comrades Captain Spencer and Major Cholmley before continuing the march. Within a few hours Cholmley would be dead.

Three miles outside Warrington the Scots came to a halt. On the road between Winwick and Newton was a strong tactical position 'in a strait passage in that lane that they made very stronge and forcible'. As another observer put it they had 'the advantage of a strong field, with a very large bank like a castle, where Oswald king of Nothumbers was formerly slain'. The site has been identified as Red Bank, and the lane, Hermitage Green Lane, near the later site of Park Cliffe Colliery. The hedges were lined with musketeers, and the Parliamentarian advanced guard were in for a nasty surprise. As Hodgson so evocatively described the result, they 'snaffled our forlorn, and put them to retreat'.[5]

Obviously a more deliberate strategy was needed to dislodge the Scots from their defensive position. It took some time for the New Model foot, including Pride's regiment, to arrive, but when they did they took on the defenders with a spirited assault. According to Cromwell,

We held them in some dispute till our Army came up; they maintaining

the Pass with great resolution for many hours; ours and theirs coming
to push of pike and very close charges, – which forced us to give ground.

Particularly stout resistance came from a Scottish regiment commanded by
'a little spark in a blue bonnet' who fought until overwhelmed and killed by
men of Pride's regiment.

Perhaps the deciding factor was intelligence. One source has it that local
people gave the parliamentarians information on the lie of the land, and whilst
the skirmishers and horse pinned the Scots from the front they guided Cromwell's infantry 'into the fields' and surrounding woods. From here they came
round the Scots threatening to outflank them. This was too demoralising, and
despite the fact that their horse appeared to be coming to their support from
the direction of Warrington the Scots began to fall back to the green near
Winwick church.[6]

Here the parliamentarians overtook them and made 'a great slaughter of
them'; others threw down their arms and ran inside the church. Baillie, doing
his best with a disintegrating command, made a fighting retreat with the
survivors in the direction of the cavalry and Warrington bridge, a route which
beckoned both escape and safety. As he arrived at Warrington he was mortified
to find both Callander and Hamilton had disappeared; a messenger was all
that greeted him with the order to make the best terms he could. He was being
told to surrender whilst his commanding officer and the horse made good their
own escape.

Turner, who says he was present at the time, described Baillie's
reaction: 'he losed much of that patience of which naturallie he was master; and beseeched any that wold to shoot him thorough the head'. It was
some time before he could regain his composure and begin to treat with
his tormentors. To add insult to injury, Turner remarked that since they
were not going to fight there was little point his remaining to be made a
prisoner. He too mounted up and left, 'carrying my wounded thigh away
with me'.

Barricading of the bridge had already begun; Baillie had the obstacle completed, and from behind it sent out Major Fleming to seek terms. Cromwell,
seeing the strength of the position, was prepared to talk, but demanded to see
Baillie himself. They met at the bridge and agreed

That all armes, ammunition, collours, and other provision of warre, be
delyvered without imbattellment to Lieut. Gen. Cromwell, or to whom he
shall appoint. That Lieut. Gen. Baylie, with all the officers and souldiers
with him, shall be prisoners of warre, and that with the consent of all the
said officers and souldiers.

That they who shall soe rander themselffes, the said Lieut. General

Cromwell shall assure them all of saiff lyves, goods and what else belongs to them, except horses.

The surrender of the foot at Warrington would rankle for years afterwards. Baillie in his own vindication was later to prepare a memorandum signed by the Scottish officers then present, including Colonels Douglas, Johnstone, Kerr, and Bunten, and Major William Douglas. This stated that the main reasons for the surrender were their abandonment by the cavalry, Hamilton's explicit order and the fact that the foot was then reduced to about 2,700, many of whom were without arms, ammunition and food. Indeed he suggested that the troops were on the point of mutiny, most refusing further orders until 'the Capitulation was closed'.[7]

Altogether 20 regiments between them surrendered more than 70 colours; there was only one cavalry cornet amongst them from Hamilton's Horse. A detailed list of the prisoners was drawn up and later published in a document entitled *Three Letters Concerning the Surrender*. By now most of the units were pitifully weak; the Duke of Hamilton's own regiment was by far the strongest to surrender, numbering 16 officers, 19 sergeants and 360 soldiers. At the other end of the scale was the tiny remnant of Argyle's Highland regiment; all the private soldiers were deserted or dead, leaving 10 officers and five sergeants as prisoners. Amongst the officers surrendering from Baillie's regiment was his own son, James. Cromwell claimed to have captured

An early nineteenth-century engraving of Winwick church, near Warrington, where survivors of the Red Bank fight sought sanctuary.

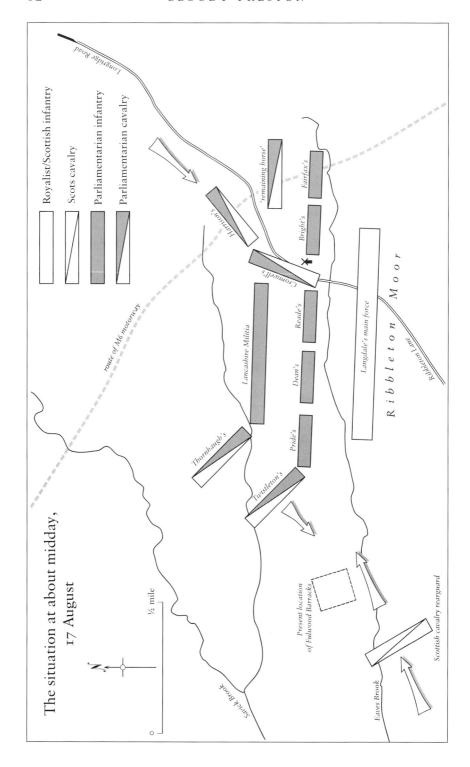

The situation at about midday,
17 August

N

½ mile

Royalist/Scottish infantry

Scots cavalry

Parliamentarian infantry

Parliamentarian cavalry

Longridge Road

route of M6 motorway

Harrison's

'remaining horse'

Fairfax's

Bright's

Cromwell's

Lancashire Militia

Reade's

Dean's

Langdale's main force

R i b b l e t o n   M o o r

Ribbleton Lane

Thornhaugh's

Pride's

Twistleton's

Savick Brook

Present location
of Fulwood Barracks

Eaves Brook

Scottish cavalry rearguard

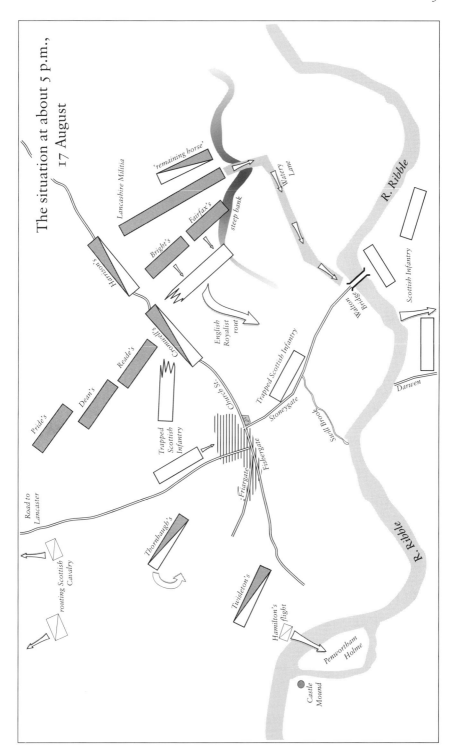

The situation at about 5 p.m., 17 August

4,000 arms. Few of the Scots would have any stomach for escape, the country people were incensed by their plundering, and they were too famished and exhausted to do more. The parliamentarian Major Cholmeley who had drunk with Hodgson and led the 'forlorn hope' was later buried in Winwick church.[8]

Local tradition would associate several other Winwick landmarks with the struggle: Gallows Croft, where it was said that a soldier or soldiers were executed for insubordination; the local post office, formerly an inn, which was occupied by the Scots; and the moat of the farm house near St Oswald's well, which yielded finds associated with 1648. Warrington Museum yet contains a spur and a small cannon ball popularly connected with the battle at Winwick. It was said that Cromwell spent that evening in lodgings in Church St, Warrington; a distinct possibility because the narrative he made of the day's events to the committee at York was written in the town.

Parliamentarian sources now put the overall 'bag' of prisoners at over 8,000, 'besides what are lurking in hedges and private places, which the country daily bring in or destroy'. One tract described the least fortunate of the Scots fugitives scattered in tiny bands, easy prey for the 'country people' who 'knock them in the head, where they meet with them'. A total of 2,000 Scots and English royalists were thought to be dead. Even so it was believed that the best part of 3,000 cavalry remained under Hamilton's orders and were heading south. Left to their own devices such a force could yet have considerable nuisance value, and so the chase was not yet over.

As the correspondent to the *Moderate Intelligencer* put it 'we are going after them with our tyred army, even beaten-out with hard duty with continual fighting for 30 miles together'. Cromwell had to admit that he was without the fresh cavalry really required for such a task, all being so 'harassed and haggled out' that the best that could be managed was an 'easy pace'. General Lambert was therefore detailed to take the vanguard in search of Hamilton, and messengers were dispatched to Lord Grey, Sir Henry Cholmely, Sir Edward Rhodes and the Governor of Stafford warning them of the remnant of the enemy force and exhorting them to gather for their interception. Cromwell's own force would make sure that Munro was no threat, and relieve Lancaster castle, which was still besieged by Tyldesley.

Hamilton appears to have been undecided as to the best plan. One possibility was to go to Chester, a Royalist stronghold of old, and thence into Wales. Another option was to attempt to outrun his adversaries, or throw them off the trail and head back for Scotland. In the end Hamilton reached Malpas in Cheshire without having made a definite decision. At Whitchurch, just within Shropshire, the local militia gathered to oppose him but dispersed when they realised General Middleton's strength in cavalry. That night Turner relates how he finally found sleep, in a hedge, and slept so soundly that the trumpets did not wake him in the morning.

The next day they crossed into Staffordshire and marched via Market Drayton. At Stone Middleton took the rearguard while the army halted. Presented with the option of heading on to Hereford, where royalists had recently been in revolt, or back to Pontefract where resistance yet continued, Hamilton finally made up his mind. His resolution was to head for Yorkshire, and thence retire into Scotland via the east coast. Morale had reached a critically low ebb; some officers drifted away, one trooper shot his own sergeant and was himself put in front of a firing squad on Hamilton's orders. Turner remarked on this incident as unusual, since the Duke was normally loath to use such discipline, and had been noticeably lax on the march. To make matters dangerous the local militias were now gaining confidence, General Middleton, in skirmishing with them, fell from his horse and was captured.[9]

The weather was still bad and 'tempestuous' when the straggling column of horse reached Uttoxeter. On the morning of 24 August the command refused to move. Major Sanderson, who was with Lambert's pursuing force, records how the parliamentarians 'lay in the fields' near the town as negotiations took place. As a complaint in the quarter sessions papers shows some of the parliamentarian troopers were billeted in the church at Bramshall, others on the farm of Richard Richardson where they and their mounts munched their way through his corn, peas, and hay 'to the value of £6'. To make things worse for Hamilton his troops were again mutinous. Callander argued with Hamilton, who was by now sick and unable to move. So it was that knowing that the end of the venture was near both Callander and Sir Marmaduke Langdale now left the tattered squadrons to their fate. Having first exchanged messages with the governor of Stafford, Hamilton at last surrendered to General Lambert on 25 August. The captured were listed in a contemporary pamphlet.[10]

The terms promised the lives of the Scots and that they would not be 'pillaged or stripped of their wearing clothes, or what they have about them, or otherwise wronged, beaten, or abused'. Hamilton was allowed to retain six servants, and the sick were granted leave to stay at Uttoxeter. The Scots signatories of the surrender document were colonels Lockhart, Foules and Turner; Lilburne, Haynes and Mainwaring signed for Parliament.

The Duke of Hamilton was now taken off via Derby and Leicester to Ashby-de-la-Zouch; in December he would be transferred to Windsor. Sir James Turner and several other officers were taken captive to Hull. Meanwhile the last few fugitives now did their best to avoid capture. Callander, with a few men, headed first for Ashbourne in Derbyshire but his party soon split up. He therefore made his way to London, and in disguise took ship for Holland.

After some discussion with Callander Langdale headed for Nottingham in the company of colonels Owen and Galliard, and Major Constable. They had thought to pass themselves off as parliamentarians, but were recognised in an ale house. Discovered in their subterfuge they were taken, and landed up in Nottingham castle. Though Langdale received 'civil usage' from his captors it was feared that the army intended to have him executed. He escaped in disguise, and after hiding in a haystack managed to make his way to his cousin's house at Houghton. Again he seemed close to apprehension and again he was forced to make his escape. One source suggests that he did this disguised as a milkmaid, complete with bonnet, then hid in a rabbit warren, and when the coast was clear he swam the Humber. Later he dressed as a clergyman and went into hiding in London; from here he took ship to the continent.[11]

7

Results of the Battle

HE PRESTON CAMPAIGN had immediate and dramatic consequences. There were still royalists in the south east, but as one
historian of Kent put it, 'Preston was the death blow of Royalism'.
Without the prospect of succour from a northern royalist army,
the southern royalists were doomed. In fact Fairfax had already suppressed
Kent, and after the battle at Maidstone in June Canterbury had surrendered.[1]

Lord Norwich with the main royalist force in the area had made for London
via Blackheath, but finding the gates shut against him had been forced to
retreat into Essex. Pinned into Colchester the royalists were closely besieged
by Fairfax, who cut off the town's water supply, and began a bombardment
with siege artillery ordered up for the purpose from the Tower. Whilst the
prospect of a Scottish victory existed Colchester would be a significant factor;
it tied up Fairfax and some of the best Parliamentarian troops, and would also
give a convenient base from which to threaten London.

On 24 August these hopes would be rudely shattered; on that day news of
Preston managed to filter through to the beleaguered garrison and three days
later they capitulated. Lords Capel and Norwich were sent prisoner to London,
but Sir Charles Lucas and Sir George Lisle faced a firing squad. It was a small
measure of the bitterness aroused by this Second Civil War and a portent of
what would follow. There were still some ships which had mutinied under
the control of Prince Charles, and later Prince Rupert, but the surrender of
Colchester effectively finished the war in England.

The same day that Colchester heard the news a delighted Derby House
committee of the parliament was writing its congratulations to Cromwell:

> We are informed of your great success and signal victory . . . which God
> gave to your forces over that great army of the Scots and their adherents
> who had invaded this kingdom, and how evidently God was pleased to
> appear for us in so great a disproportion of numbers. It is alike easy to Him
> to save with many or with few where He will own the cause . . . We do
> also return you thanks for your great resolution to engage them with so
> small a number, and for your good conduct and effectual pursuing your

first victory to the total dispersing of all their foot. And we desire you to give thanks from us to all your officers and soldiers for their great resolution and valiant carriage as in all their other services so in this a very especial manner, of whom as we desire to have an esteem suitable to their great merit, so we have a very tender resentment of their wants.

The bearers of the news to parliament had been Major Berry and Captain Sexby, who received respectively £200 and £100 for their troubles. It was a handsome reward, but also an amazing feat of endurance since they must have covered 200 miles in about four days. Whilst tacitly admitting the army's lack of pay the committee went on to exhort Cromwell to finish the job with the 'rendition of the towns of Berwick and Carlisle'.[2] Captain Pitson of the Lord General's regiment arrived at parliament a day or two later, burdened with a hundred captured Scottish colours, cornets and guidons. On the 25th he made a 'verbal relation' to the honourable members of the climactic battle. He was given £100 for his pains, but more importantly was finally paid the £452 10s. which had been owing in arrears and disbursements since his days as 'Scoutmaster' to Sir William Waller.

Neither Sir Thomas Tyldesley nor Sir Philip Musgrave were actually on the field at Preston. Nevertheless both were important actors in the campaign as a whole. After the battle Sir Philip was forced to retreat on Carlisle by the approach of Ashton and the Lancashire forces. Fearing that Carlisle would surrender he struck out for Appleby. From here, in the company of Tyldesley, who had been forced to desist in his attempt to take Lancaster castle, he could view with dismay the steadily deteriorating situation. Besieged by Ashton in a 'place not tenable, nor vitteld for above six weeks' they were forced to capitulate.

The terms were reasonable; other ranks and junior officers were free to go so long as they laid down their arms and agreed to obey the ordinances of parliament, Colonels were given six months in which to leave the country. The chief officers surrendering in addition to Musgrave and Tyldesley were Sir Robert Strickland and Sir William Huddlestone; the total number of Colonels and Lieutenant Colonels was 24, and there were 82 lesser officers, an officer corps which appears to have been swollen by survivors of Preston. The common soldiery numbered a little over 1,000. Five pieces of ordnance and 1,000 arms were also given up. Tyldesley would die bravely three years later, in the service of the new king, at Wigan Lane.[3]

Cromwell had marched north after Preston and easily driven Munro, who had been in the Kirkby Lonsdale area, back to Scotland. Sir Thomas Tyldesley had attempted to persuade Munro to remain, but despite his failure to become seriously engaged he was no longer prepared to risk his small force. By September General Lambert had rejoined Cromwell, and now the 'engager'

Sir Thomas Tyldesley, by an unknown artist. Tyldesley was one of the most active and able English northern royalists; his presence at Preston with an extra regiment could have bought a little time for the Anglo-Scottish army. He would die as he lived, in the service of the monarchy, at Wigan Lane in the Third Civil War of 1651. (*National Portrait Gallery*)

junta in Scotland themselves faced a rebellion in Clydesdale and Galloway. The new Model Army now advanced into Scotland and completed the coup; Cromwell was welcomed in Edinburgh by the new ruling party. The peace treaty surrendered Berwick and Carlisle back to Parliament, and Munro was packed off back to Ireland.[4]

Such was the immediate effect of Preston, which had been the climax and deciding battle of the war. It is also arguable that the campaign had further reaching and even more important consequences. Throughout the summer of 1648 Charles I had been effectively a powerless bystander securely locked up at Carisbrooke castle on the Isle of Wight; two escape attempts, in March and May 1648 respectively, had failed. He had been a prime mover in the tragedy by his refusal to negotiate seriously and by his willingness to enter the engagement with the Scots, but once the storm had been unleashed there was little that he could do to influence events until the military campaign had worked its way out.

Now negotiations were to go on, but this time the parliament was not going to be fobbed off with prevarication, nor would they be prepared to countenance a solution which left the king power and scope to begin new wars. The parliamentarian commissioners sought agreement on four major points in the treaty at Newport: the retraction of all proclamations against parliament made in the Civil Wars; the abolition of Episcopacy; the control of the militia; and an endorsement on the Irish question. Given assurances on these basic matters Charles would remain a king, but a very different sort of monarch to that which he had been in 1642. Those who had defeated him could feel a form of security in their actions, and Charles would be relatively powerless having relinquished the means to make war, and effectively having abandoned both his power and his principle in terms of religion.

To expect a man such as Charles to sign a document like this was optimistic to say the least, but in September 1648 while the loose ends of the war were still untied, the king gave some reason to believe that an accommodation could be reached. Significant concessions were made, but the totality of the package was unlikely to be accepted. Next Charles demanded that the negotiation be removed to London and made with the full parliament; at the same time he began a theological debate on the role of Bishops, and their biblical justification. The commissioners pressurised him for more speed, and whilst publicly amenable, in secret the king began to plan for another escape attempt.[5]

Whilst the parliament may have been prepared to allow this charade to go on longer, there were many in the army who were not. The army's 'Remonstrance' to the Parliament had gone unsatisfied, and there were still within the ranks of the military men of a 'Levelling' persuasion. The country was still far from calm with rumours of disturbance in Pembroke and London, and there were many soldiers unpaid. The army now relieved Governor Hammond at Carisbrooke of his duties. On 6 December troops of the New Model under command of Henry Ireton took over guard of the parliament house from the local London 'Trained Bands'. The next day the honourable members found their entrance to the house blocked by Colonel Pride; his orders were to exclude all those who were known opponents of the army.

'Pride's Purge' was unconstitutional by any definition of the term, but it opened up possibilities only dimly comprehended until that moment. Charles had already been moved to the mainland at Hurst Castle; now he was escorted up to Windsor. In the words which Eikon Basiliske put into the mouth of Charles I, 'They think my kingdomes on earth too little to entertain at once both them and me'.[6]

The Newport treaty was, with hindsight, the last real opportunity left to

Charles the martyr, from the 1649 'Eikon Basiliske'. The Preston campaign helped
to seal his fate, and bring about the change in opinion which made a republic
possible. (*Private collection*)

the king. At Windsor Charles had one very brief and poignant meeting with
Hamilton in the courtyard as the guards rushed him past. According to one
account the Duke was able only to utter 'My dear master . . .' from a kneeling
position in the mud, and Charles to reply 'I have been so indeed to you', before
they were parted. It was a far cry indeed from the victorious celebration which
had been envisaged. At Whitehall, meanwhile, parliament was laying the
groundwork for the king's trial. He was accused of 'a wicked design totally
to subvert the ancient and fundamental laws and liberties of this nation, and
in their place to introduce an arbitrary and tyrannical government', a traitorous
and malicious plan, carried out by means of fire and the sword. To bring the
king to trial involved the jumping of several constitutional hurdles; and quite
a few who had gone to war against the kings 'evil councillors' in 1642, in the
name of 'King and Parliament', were loath to take not only such a drastic
step, but such a leap in the dark in terms of government.

Despite protests from the Scots commissioners, and French and Spanish representatives, and Fairfax's obvious unwillingness to play a part when the king was actually in Whitehall, Charles was brought to trial. He was condemned to death and executed on 30 January 1649. Charles had died, at least indirectly, because of the failure at Preston. So started eleven years of England without a king. Within a few days acts of parliament were passed abolishing the monarchy and the house of Lords. The way was open first to a 'Commonwealth', and then to a 'Protectorate', with a lord protector who could variously be interpreted as a king in all but name, or as the first army leader in English history, who was not a prince or magnate, to seize civil power.[7]

If the fortunes of King Charles I took a turn for the worst as a result of Preston, the battle was also a turning point for Cromwell. Though the civil wars are sometimes thought of in the popular imagination as a struggle between the two personalities, nothing could be further from the truth. In 1642 Cromwell had been as near to total obscurity as a member of the House of Commons could be; in the first years of the first civil war he was a relatively junior officer, and only in 1644 did he come to prominence as a lieutenant general of cavalry. It is arguable that 1648 confirmed his superior military ability, and gave him his first significant opportunities for political power, opened up by Pride's Purge, the death of the king and Fairfax's unwillingness to take to the political arena.

That Cromwell had demonstrated both good generalship and a mastery of public relations in the Preston campaign is undeniable. To win from an unpromising position he had employed not only single-minded determination but a number of important military principles. Arguably the most significant was concentration; in the face of a potential inferiority of numbers he had joined his force to that of Lambert and the local militia, and maintained them in close proximity during the vital period leading up to the battle of 17 August. More than that strategic concentration he managed to achieve a tactical concentration at the vital spot. Faced with Langdale's small force he had used most of his army on a relatively narrow front, and despite determined resistance had pressed home his localised advantage in numbers. Cromwell did everything in his power to maintain the initiative. From the morning of 17 August onward all the moves were dictated by his agenda, and once the royalist-Scottish army were off balance constant pressure meant that they could only react. Pursuit and exploitation were the keynotes which prevented Winwick being a Scottish victory.

Also important was Cromwell's use of intelligence. In this matter the Scots played into his hands, their own intelligence gathering was poor, and as a 'foreign' force plundering the countryside were unlikely to get much help from the people of Lancashire. On the parliamentarian side there is good evidence of organised intelligence gathering activity by both Cromwell and Lambert. Major Sanderson seems specifically to have been employed as an intelligence officer, or 'Scout master' in contemporary parlance. Accounts submitted in June 1648 show his use of paid spies; Thomas Gooley was rewarded with 5s for 'going into the enemies quarters near Berwick' after the town's capture, Others were paid varying sums up to 12s to watch the enemy's movements, and estimate their strength.[8]

In terms of public relations and Cromwell's personal standing Preston was also a triumph. His letters to parliament describing the campaign and the victory were modest in the sense that they ascribed the glory to God, but they subtly magnified Oliver Cromwell. The strength of the enemy is always listed as its greatest possible, his own army at its minimum. His name was always in the minds of the parliament and his reports put him on a level with Fairfax, his general. Cromwell's conduct of the aftermath demonstrated similar skill, as he proved able to exploit rebellion in Scotland in a way that the Scots army had proved signally unable in England. Whilst Pride's Purge was taking place Cromwell was in the background; when it was over he was there to take advantage of its fruits. When Fairfax shied away from the killing of the king, Cromwell had no such scruple. Cromwell would go on to be the dominating figure of mid seventeenth-century English history, a man who mastered confusion with overwhelming conviction. He would reach his apogee in 1653 when, after experiment and exasperation with various forms of Government he would become Lord Protector of England, Scotland and Ireland. To his detractors he was a bigot and a hypocrite, a man who heard God's voice and purpose solely in his own; a man who had helped to murder the king, only to become king in all but name himself. He could safely be blamed for everything from the Irish problem to the despoliation of churches and castles.

For his partisans Cromwell the hero was almost a martyr who championed the people and the liberties of parliament against a tyrannical king, and at last brought strength and peace out of anarchy. His power as an icon for his period is difficult to exaggerate, and even at the time of his death in 1658 it was not apparent that there was anyone who could satisfactorily fill the vacuum created by his passing. With the passage of time the efforts of his son Richard, and even of John Lambert, appear like minnows swimming against a tide. So pervasive was his memory that the new regime at the Restoration thought it necessary to dig him up and execute him along with other regicides. If history still has not found a definitive niche for Cromwell, it can at least be said that if his nerve had failed at Preston the whole course of British history would have been different.

If Cromwell made capital from his victory, Preston had been the Duke of Hamilton's Armageddon. He followed Charles I to the block in front of the

Parliament House at Westminster, with lords Holland and Capel, in March 1649. As he was effectively a 'foreign' prisoner of war who had surrendered on terms this was harsh, but Hamilton was also Earl of Cambridge, and convicted of treason. In truth the Scottish commander's abilities as a general had been exposed in the summer of 1648 as pretty slender.

Hamilton's first obvious mistake was his failure to liaise with his many potential allies; within England were Langdale, Musgrave and Tyldesley in the north, in the south were the Kent royalists, later led by Lord Norwich. There were anti-parliament forces in Wales, and potential pockets of sympathy in Hereford, Yorkshire and Cornwall. In the navy were men on the point of mutiny, and Prince Charles could be expected to lend support, and tone, to the proceedings, from the continent. Hamilton's actions coordinated with none of them and in the event only Langdale was able to fight alongside the Scots; one gets the impression that this was more Langdale's common sense than any positive indicator regarding Hamilton.

Also likely to be a problem from the outset was political instability within Scotland itself. Argyle, David Leslie and others were against the venture, with only a small majority in favour in the Scottish parliament. Problems with recruiting compounded the point; earliest projections and requirements looked for an army of 40,000. Realistically this was scaled down to 20,000, and the probable total achieved is more likely to have been a little over 15,000, plus Munro's small 'New Scots' contingent from Ireland. The evidence regarding plunder and the statements of other Scottish generals suggests that the supply situation was poor. Given these difficulties it is dubious whether the invasion should have gone ahead at this juncture, and indeed Lord Lanark had recommended postponement.

If some of the strategic and political issues were outside Hamilton's control the same cannot be said of the tactics. If Cromwell practised skilful concentration at what the Germans might call a 'Schwerpunkt', the Scots were hopelessly dissipated. Munro might as well have been on the moon for all the impact his force had on the battle of Preston, and Middleton's main force of cavalry was simply too far out in front to return in time to any action involving Baillie's infantry.

Scouting and intelligence were at best indifferent, and research has as yet failed to discover anything approximating to the New Model's tried and tested system in which spies were the first line, dragoon and cavalry patrols the second, and a thick line of skirmishers or the 'forlorn hope' the third. When reliable information was provided by Langdale the wrong conclusion was drawn. The historian Hume even went so far as to suggest that cooperation with Langdale could have been deliberately lukewarm due to religious difference, an inference which might also be drawn from Sir Philip Musgrave's relation. Hamilton also seems to have had a less than perfect understanding with his subordinate commanders. As leader he should have been in a position to control bickering between Callander and Baillie, between Callander and Turner, and between several officers and himself. Councils of war should have heard opinions in private and resolved their differences, leading to definite objectives. Bishop Burnet, taking the kindest possible view, remarked on Hamilton's personal bravery, and noted that his real fault was 'yielding too much' to others. Turner's best epitaph was that he had excellent personal qualities, was courteous, affable, humane but unfortunate.[9]

Hamilton's subordinates fared better in the aftermath of the campaign. Callander had his estates confiscated but survived the turmoils of Cromwell's protectorate and political upheaval in Scotland. He was politically active after 1660, and died in 1674. Baillie lived, and later went to the Hague and the court of Charles II. He died in 1662, and though of fair military ability is better remembered as a presbyterian divine than a soldier. Middleton went on to a rich and varied future which demonstrated his resilience and persistence, if no superlative military skill. He escaped from captivity and fought at Worcester, under Charles II, in 1651. This led to his recapture and imprisonment in the Tower; from here he escaped, apparently dressed in his wife's clothes. Fighting Monck in Scotland he was defeated at Dalnaspidal in 1654, but again survived to join Charles II on the continent. He prospered at the Restoration becoming commander in chief in Scotland, but lost his position as the result of a bribery scandal. He died after a fall when governor of Tangier in 1673.[10]

Sir James Turner, opinionated chronicler of the Scottish command in 1648, also survived. Being a man of means he paid for his own captivity, first under close confinement at Hull, and later under a more relaxed regime at Newcastle. He went into exile in November 1649, and returned to Scotland the next year. In the Worcester campaign he was adjutant general to the infantry and was again captured. This time he succeeded in escaping to France, and was then employed by Charles II on various European missions before taking service with the Danish army. Returning to Scotland after the Restoration he was given command of forces in the south west of the country. His rough attitude to justice may have helped spark the Pentland rising of 1666. In the 1670s Turner was in correspondence with Bishop Burnet and others: this may explain to some degree the points of similarity between Burnet's account of 1648, and Sir James' own memoirs. Turner is perhaps best remembered for his *Pallas Armata*, written in the early 1670s, but published in 1683. This work, subtitled 'Military Essayes of the Ancient Grecian, Roman, and Modern Art of War', and dedicated to James Duke of York, later king James II, gives the best insight available into Turner's own abilities.

First, and most obviously, Turner drew inspiration from classical models.

PALLAS ARMATA.

Military Essayes

Of the ANCIENT

GRECIAN,

ROMAN,

AND

MODERN

ART of WAR.

Written in the Years 1670 and 1671.

By Sir JAMES TURNER, Knight.

LONDON,

Printed by *M. W.* for Richard Chiswell at the *Rose* and *Crown* in
S. *Paul's* Church-yard.   MDCLXXXIII.

The title page from Sir James Turner's military textbook, 'Pallas Armata'.

In this he was a traditionalist, as similar parallels were drawn as far back as the early Renaissance; it was also an approach used most famously by Machiavelli, about 1520, in his *Art of War*. More alarming are some of the ideas espoused in Turner's essays on 'Modern' war. Many of the points of view are very old fashioned. Turner still thinks that the pike is queen of the battlefield, still thinks that full armour is desirable, and, most remarkably, thinks that the longbow ought to be reintroduced. The last time that such a suggestion was seriously debated in military circles had been the last quarter of the sixteenth century.

Pallas Armata also gives some revealing remarks on intelligence gathering. All men are regarded as liars and not to be trusted, as 'a fool or a knave may ruin you if you believe either of them'. Suspected enemy spies should be killed out of hand, and preferably tortured, not so much to give information as to discourage others. Your own troops should only be sent short distances to gather news, and normally in odd numbered parties. The surest way to get any information worth hearing is to corrupt and bribe enemy garrison commanders, and general's staffs. It is difficult to escape the conclusion that despite long experience, and several salutary lessons, that Turner remained a complete reactionary in matters military. He is believed to have died about 1685.[11]

Marmaduke Lord Langdale, who had again proved himself a competent and determined general during the campaign, was lucky to survive with his life after Preston. At the time Hamilton was executed Langdale was condemned to death in his absence by Parliament. Prince Charles, already declared Charles II by the Scots, was more appreciative, giving him a gift of £500 in June 1649. Lord Lauderdale wrote to him congratulating him on his escape from 'those bloody rogues who have murthered our king and our friends'. Langdale continued faithful in the Royal cause, and visited the Isle of Man to assist the royalist Earl of Derby. The 1650s were spent in penurious exile; in theory there was a pension from the French but little evidence of its payment. In 1654 there was strange talk that Langdale would be called upon to lead a 'Leveller' army in England against Cromwell. Perhaps fortunately history never actually called upon these weird bedfellows to fight together. By the end of the decade Langdale was frequently ill with gout, and was staying at the Abbey of Lambspring in Westphalia. His fortunes finally turned with the Restoration; he was appointed Lord Lieutenant for the West Riding of Yorkshire, regained his estate at Holme-on-Spalding-Moor, and at last returned to see his family. His joy was shortlived as he died in August 1661.[12]

General Lambert, sometimes referred to as 'Cromwell's Understudy', had fought a brilliant campaign at Preston, and may be justly thought of as one of the heros or villains of the hour depending on standpoint. For several weeks, and with a tiny force, Lambert had fenced and skirmished with Scots and

Royalists. He had delayed and perplexed them, gathered intelligence, and extricated himself when it seemed likely that his command could be crushed by overwhelming odds. He had managed to join up with Cromwell, fit easily into the command, and then play an important and intelligent role both in the main battle at Preston and in the pursuit. His cavalry rode further and fought longer than any other, and was there to take Hamilton's final surrender. Cromwell took most of the glory and Lambert does not seem to have begrudged it.

After Preston Lambert was one of the most active generals in the Commonwealth's army. In March 1649, in an uneasy postscript to the Preston campaign, Ashton's Lancashire troops refused to disband. Lambert was ordered to use force against them if necessary; but in the end they gave up for the most part without a fight, and also surrendered Clitheroe castle which Parliament directed to be destroyed. The only exceptions were one or two renegade companies, especially that of captain Bamber, which had been stealing horses under colour of being directed to proceed to Ireland for service. This activity was eventually halted by Colonel Duckenfield.

Generals Lambert and Desborough caricatured as puppet masters of Oliver Cromwell's son Richard, c.1659 (*Private collection*)

Lambert fought in the Scotch campaigns, and was especially prominent at Dunbar in 1650, where he was second in command. In a strange replay of the Preston campaign Lambert shadowed the Scottish invasion of 1651, and fought at the battle of Worcester. His political influence and ambitions increased in the 1650s; during the 'Barebones' Parliament he was earmarked for the Lord Deputyship of Ireland but the post was abolished. He then became President of the Council of State, and helped to establish Cromwell's Protectorate in which he was one of the councillors. With the death of Cromwell in 1658 Lambert became identified as one of the chief power brokers, if not actually a potential successor. In the event Richard Cromwell was briefly the new Lord Protector, but after his deposition in 1659, Lambert, who was by now associated with the 'fifth monarchists', first helped to restore, and then drove out the 'Rump' Parliament. He attempted to impose a new constitution of two chambers with a Council of State. At one point there was even talk that Lambert's daughter should marry Charles II.

All these plans were derailed by General Monck's intervention; Lambert attempted to take the field against him but his forces collapsed when the old Lord General, Fairfax, appeared out of retirement to support Monck. Lambert surrendered and landed up in the Tower. From here he made a remarkable escape but was only at liberty for a few days before being recaptured. He was condemned to death, but was reprieved by Charles II who told the Earl of Clarendon that he was 'weary of hanging'. For about eight years he was exiled to Guernsey, but was taken to an Islet in Plymouth Sound in 1670. Here he painted, studied and worked in the gardens. For a total of more than 20 years Lambert remained a prisoner; he outlived most who had been present at Preston, but in a sad end to a remarkable career, he died, probably of pneumonia, in 1683. One source has it that he died 'devoid of his reason', if so he can only have been without his wits a short time, for in the late 1670s he had been swopping mathematical problems with correspondents, and shortly prior to his death he was still receiving visitors whom he was careful to greet in his best attire.[13]

Undoubtedly those faring worst from the Preston campaign were the common soldiery; the least lucky could not even expect a marked grave. Regiments and companies had their own muster lists but there was no central registry, and the defeated especially would have been interred in haste and anonymity. Around the town of Preston itself odd bones and shot have been turned up as far apart as Killing Sough farm, north of Fulwood, and Pear Tree farm south of the Ribble, yet there has been no archeological study and no definite identification of grave pits. Care for the wounded was minimal, and although good surgeons had better knowledge than is often appreciated, the ordinary soldier was unlikely to be able to afford their ministrations. Prospects for those disabled were very slender. The lack of anaesthesia at the time is also often remarked, but this was perhaps the least of the problem since it was impossible to miss that which was yet to be invented. At least as important were the fevers, infections and septicaemia which would have gone virtually unchecked; epidemics followed in the wake of the armies.

The private soldiers had also proved something; and this was that the victory of the New Model in 1645 and 1646 had been no freak, or simply by virtue of overwhelming numbers. During the Preston campaign they had shown the ability of parliament's army to march and fight against overwhelming odds and win. They would prove it again and again, in Scotland, and Ireland, and against foreign powers. It would all demonstrate the power and the dangers of a standing army, and the similarities of the rule of the Major Generals, and of the Protector, with modern military dictatorship, have already been pointed out. While the 'standing army' would become a centre of debate in the second half of the seventeenth-century 'local' and part time armies, like the militia and the 'Associations', would be steadily eclipsed. Within a hundred years part time soldiers would be widely regarded as a joke, a refuge of those who had no wish to be dragooned into the 'real' army, or as a plaything of the nobility. To some extent it was a mirror of how power would pass progressively from the provinces to the centre; but it left a distinctive mark on English attitudes both to politics and the army.

Exact casualty figures are notoriously difficult to establish for Civil War battles, not only through deliberate misrepresentations, but through ignorance and confusion. Outside the New Model individual regiments had their own coat colours, there were no identity discs, and the slain were often stripped of arms, coats and breeches as well as valuables. The defeated seem to have had no leisure to compile statistics, but Cromwell suggests that the Scots and Royalists lost 1,000 dead at Preston and the immediate pursuit, a further 1,000 at Winwick and its environs, and about 9,000 captured: to which should be added the 1,000 taken at Appleby and up to 3,000 more taken prisoner or disarmed in the skirmishing and flight through four counties from Warrington to Uttoxeter. All are suspiciously round figures, most obviously inaccurate because they omit any calculation of the wounded. If Cromwell slightly exaggerated the dead, we should think of adding at least 2,000 wounded, and even if the prisoner figures are slightly inflated, an estimate of 11,000 to 12,000 seems wholly credible. Such calculations would seem to leave something about 5,000 Scots and Royalists unaccounted for; but this is quite reasonable since we know that most of Munro's command made it back to Scotland and that a percentage of Hamilton's army fled north rather than south after Preston, and some at least evaded capture. A handful at least appear to have been slaughtered by country folk. It is also highly likely that a small percentage of

Langdale's men were able to discard their arms and make their way home, or take refuge with royalist sympathisers, being less conspicuous than the Scots.

The fate of prisoners was determined both by luck, rank, and origin. Few if any apart from Hamilton were executed, though a good number perished by other means. In one instance 1,500 were rounded up and kept in St Thomas's church Chapel-en-le-Frith; of these 44 died of wounds or disease between 14 and 30 September, and a further 15 whilst being marched to Chester. Other fugitives were lynched by the Lancastrians they had despoiled, but the Royalists from Appleby got away virtually scot free. A parliamentary committee assembled to determine the disposal of prisoners decided that Scots who had been conscripted would be sent home

A much decayed basket hilted sword found at Woodplumpton, almost certainly an authentic relic of the 1648 campaign. (*Private collection*)

if they promised never to invade England again, whilst volunteers would be sent as slaves to Barbados. In the eyes of some the fate of the Scots deported was poetic justice; those who had sold their king in 1646 were themselves sold for 2s. apiece in 1648.[14] Some are even said to have landed up at galley slaves in Venice.

The Parliamentarians' own losses are also difficult to assess. When parliament decreed a day of thanksgiving they stated that only 'one hundred at the most' had been killed. Cromwell minimised the loss by mentioning specifically only senior officers but did admit there were 'many' wounded. We do know that Colonel Thornhaugh, Lieutenant Colonel Cowell, and Major Cholmley, were all dead. Since these are the senior officers required for a regiment, and the struggle against Langdale and Baillie was hard fought and protracted, it would be most surprising if the total were less than 500 killed and wounded.

The ordinary people of Lancashire had also lost as a result of the campaign; some were certainly killed outright in the confusion, but most suffered in less dramatic ways. At one end of the scale was Nicholas Taylor of Warton who remained unpaid for an ox, at the other were widows, orphans, and the people of Wigan and Ashton who complained that

The seventeenth-century image of the plundering soldier. The Scots are said literally to have stolen the cooking pots from poor men's houses.

Through them the two great bodies of the late Scottish and English armies passed, and in their very bowels was that great fighting, bloud shed, and breaking. In this county hath the plague of pestilence been ranging these three years upwards, occasioned chiefly by the wars. There is a very great scarcity and dearth of all provisions . . . and . . . many families that pine away at home, not having faces to beg.

Although the Scots had been the worst predators there were also burdens imposed by Parliamentarians. A few days after Preston a fresh regiment bearing black colours had arrived from Durham, and according to one local these were 'the most theevish companies that ever the country was pestered with during the war'. Billeted in the Kirkham area they were given £100 for three days quarter, but nonetheless marauded the parish plundering and stealing.[15]

Very unusually the House of Commons was moved to order that all voluntary contributions given on the next thanksgiving day, in the parishes of England and Wales, be given to Lancashire. The money was to be distributed by the Justices of the Peace, half for wounded soldiers, half for the relief of sick and destitute civilians.[16]

What was given with one hand was likely to be taken with the other at a future date. Although the ordinary people had little to give, former royalist officers were a target for fines and 'sequestrations'. It has been estimated that almost three quarters of the Royalist gentry of Lancashire lost through property confiscation or financial penalties at the end of the wars. Even in 1649 John Allen of Bury was moved to remark that the laws had become 'New Modelised and Cromwellysed'. Most gentry were not however completely ruined, and in certain instances property was bought by relatives and kept within the old ruling families. Although the Civil Wars, and especially the bloody Preston campaign, had shocked and shaken Lancashire society, and brought change in its wake, there seemed to be certain fundamentals that could not be altered, even by fire and the sword.[17]

Appendix I

The Armies

Scottish and Royalist Forces

Scottish Army – Hamilton

Commander in chief	James Duke of Hamilton
Lieutenant General	James Livingstone 1st Earl of Callander
Lieutenant General of Horse	John Middleton
Lieutenant General of Foot	William Baillie
Adjutant General	Sir James Turner
General of Artillery	Alexander Hamilton

Cavalry (Middleton's command)

	approximate strength
Hamilton's Life Guard	150
Barclay's Horse	180*
College of Justice Regiment	180*
Cranston's Horse	280
Crawford-Lindsay's Horse	180*
Dalhousie's Horse	200
Dudhope's Horse	80*
Dunfermline's Horse	180*
Erroll's Horse	80*
Forbes' Troop	24*
Frendraught's Horse	80*
Garthland's Horse	80*
Home's Horse	80*
Innes' Horse	180
Kenmure's Horse	80*
Lanark's Horse	80*
Lauderdale's Horse	100*
Livingstone's Horse	100*
Middleton's Troop	80

Earl Marischal's Horse	80
Montgomery's Horse	80*
Sinclair's Horse	80*
Traquair's Horse	600
William Urry's Horse	80
Total	3214

Normal Scottish cavalry organisation was a three-troop 180-man regiment, the troops being commanded by the colonel, lieutenant colonel, and major respectively.

Lambert and Burnet put Hamilton's cavalry strength at about 4,000 so it is likely that the above list is incomplete. The asterisks indicate units which although probably involved in the Preston campaign are not mentioned by name in the various contemporary accounts of the battle. The very small size of each individual unit is readily apparent, and whilst numerous in total the force is certain to have suffered organisational problems. Taking into account the contemporary estimates, allowing for sickness and desertion, and noting Furgol's work on the Scottish records office papers cited in the *Regimental History of the Covenanting Armies*, it seems reasonable to suggest that the total number of cavalry available in Middleton's command on 17 August 1648 was about 3,500.

Infantry (Baillie's Command)

	Nominal strength ordered to be raised
Marquis of Argyle's Regiment	800
General of the Artillery's Regiment	800
Earl of Atholl's Regiment	800
General William Baillie's Regiment	800
Lord Bargany's Regiment	900
Earl of Callander's Regiment (intended 1,500)	1,000
James Lord Carnegie's Regiment	1,000
Colonel Richard Douglas' Regiment	1,000
Sir James Drummond of Mechanie's Regiment	800
William Earl of Dumfries' Regiment	600
Sir Alexander Frazer of Philorth's Firelocks	200
Sir John Grey's Regiment	800
Duke of Hamilton's Regiment	1,500
James Earl of Home's Regiment	1,200
Colonel George Keith's Regiment	600
Alexander Earl of Kellie's Regiment	750
Colonel Harry Maule's Regiment	600

Robert Lord Roxburgh's Regiment	1,000
James Earl of Tullibardine's Regiment	800
Colonel Sir James Turner's Regiment	800
John Lord Hay of Yester's Foot	1,200
Theoretical maximum	17,950

Despite this very impressive nominal total, the numbers actually raised, and used at Preston were a good deal lower. The infantry were arranged into ad hoc 'brigades' which would have made the handling of such a large force with under-strength regiments easier. Callandar's regiment was detached for garrison duty at Carlisle. Cromwell claims that Hamilton's infantry were 12,000 strong, Lambert and Burnet state more conservatively that the figure was 'about' 10,000. If under recruitment, sickness and desertion accounted for a 30 percent reduction and Callander's regiment is discounted it would have left 12,065. It therefore seems reasonable to estimate that the total infantry available to Baillie on 17 August 1648 were about 11,500. Since the army's own papers appear to have been lost at Preston it is unlikely that a more exact statement will be found. Each regiment would therefore have numbered between 400 and 600 on average.

Artillery (Alexander Hamilton)

The artillery component of the Scottish army is perhaps the most controversial since most modern authorities have taken at face value Turner's statement that there was no 'Train of Artillery'. This is directly contradicted by two contemporary pamphlets, and an eighteenth-century source. Perhaps the most likely explanation is that the Scots did have approximately 20 guns, light pieces and leather guns, which accompanied their infantry, but no siege pieces or separate 'train'.

Hamilton's Army: Totals

Cavalry	3,500
Infantry	11,500
guns	20 light pieces

Munro's 'Irish' force

The detailed composition of Munro's force remains a mystery. What is known is that the army in Ulster intended to send in excess of 3,000 men to the aid of the English Royalists and Engager army. Burnet states that it was agreed that the expeditionary force should consist of 1,200 horse and 2,100 foot.

Whatever number was finally dispatched from Ireland about 300 of Dalyel's regiment were captured on route by Parliamentarian warships. It is thought that Munro's infantry were drawn from six regiments and that his cavalry were organised in 12 troops. Despite not fighting a pitched battle with the New Model Munro's force was much depleted and weakened by the campaign, not least by opposition and obstruction within Scotland. The main body, when it encamped at Campsie and Monyabroch at the end of August, totalled only 362 cavalry and 1,099 foot.

Commander	Major General George Munro
Cavalry	12 troops of about 80 each
Infantry	6 Regiments each of about 300.

Given the smallness of the force it is likely that the infantry were operated as a single brigade.

Munro's Army: Totals

Cavalry	960
Infantry	1,800

Sir Marmaduke Langdale's English Royalist Army

Langdale estimated his own force at Preston to consist of 3,000 foot and 600 horse. Sir Philip Musgrave stated that Langdale initially commanded 1,200 horse but that 500 of these were sent to Northumberland under Sir Richard Tempest and there defeated by Colonel Thomas Lilburne's men. Cromwell again gave the enemy a high total, estimating Langdale's cavalry at 1,500 and his foot at 2,500. Assuming that neither Langdale nor Musgrave would have purposefully overstated the Royalist strength, but that Cromwell had a vested interest in doing so, it is reasonable to work on the basis of about 3,000 foot and 700 horse.

Commander in Chief	Sir Marmaduke Langdale
Cavalry	Sir Philip Musgrave's Regiment
Plus up to eight small troops raised by the infantry colonels	
Total	700

Infantry

Sir Philip Musgrave's Regiment
Sir Henry Bellingham's Regiment

Sir Patricius Curwen's Regiment
Sir Edward Musgrave's Regiment
Sir William Huddlestone's Regiment
Sir Henry Featherston's Regiment
Colonel Chater's Regiment
Colonel Carleton's Regiment
Average strength 375,   total 3000

Sir Marmaduke Langdale's Army: Totals

Cavalry   700
Infantry   3,000

Sir Philip Musgrave's English Royalist Force

Little is known about the precise composition of the force commanded by Sir Philip Musgrave, save that it must have been very small, totalling not much more than 1,200 horse and foot, even including Colonel Tyldesley's men and assorted stragglers at Appleby, after the battle of Preston. According to Musgrave's own Relation when his advanced guard first seized Carlisle it had only 16 men, including his kinsman 'Mr Denton' and John Eglanby esq. From Carlisle he collected 100 foot, 50 'ill armed' horse and 3 'great iron guns'. Sir Philip's own regiments of horse and foot were at Preston under Langdale. At the time of the battle on 17 August it is therefore dubious whether Musgrave and Tyldesley could have had more than 1,000 men each under arms in Lancashire, Yorkshire and Cumberland, plus a few hundred garrison troops. Some idea of numbers is given by the fact that Carlisle was promised 500 muskets by the Scots.

Commander   Colonel Sir Philip Musgrave
                      (His own regiments absent at Preston)
Colonel   Sir Thomas Tyldesley
Colonel   Sir Robert Strickland
Colonel   Henry Wogan
Colonel   George Denton
Lt Colonel   Roscarick, Governor of Appleby
possibly others with minor commands

Sir Philip Musgrave's Forces: Total

Cavalry   500
Infantry   1,500

also Callanders regiment at Carlisle
Guns   perhaps 10 garrison pieces.

Approximate grand total of all Royalist and Scottish Forces in Lancashire theatre of war, 17 August 1648

Cavalry   5,660
Infantry   18,300
                          Total   23,960
Guns   30
(perhaps only 20 of which field guns)

Parliamentarian Forces

Lieutenant General Cromwell's Detachment, New Model Army

Commander   Lieutenant General Oliver Cromwell

Cavalry

Nominal Strength

Cromwell's Regiment of Horse:
Known officers: Major Blackmore, Capt. Joseph Wallington,
Capt. John Spenser, Capt. Edward Sexby   480
Harrison's Regiment of Horse, Colonel Thomas Harrison
(wounded 17 July)
Known officers; Major William Rainborowe, Capt. John Peck,
Capt. Whitehead, Capt. Henry Cromwell, Capt. Winthrop,
Cornet Wentworth Day   480
Twisleton's Regiment of Horse, Colonel Philip Twisleton:
Known officers: Major James Berry, Capt. Hezekiah Haynes   480
Capt. Henry Markham, Capt. John Nelthorp,
Capt. Owen Cambridge, Capt. Bushey, Capt. Pearte.
Thornhaugh's Regiment of Horse, Colonel Francis Thornhaugh:
Known officers: Major Thomas Saunders, Capt. John Wright,
Capt. Philip Pendock, Capt George Palmer, Capt. Richard Creed,
Quartermaster Richard Franck   480
Scroope's Regiment of Horse, Colonel Adrian Scroope
(absent in south):
Known officers: Major Barton. Three troops   240
Okey's Regiment of Dragoons Two companies   200
theoretical maximum   2360

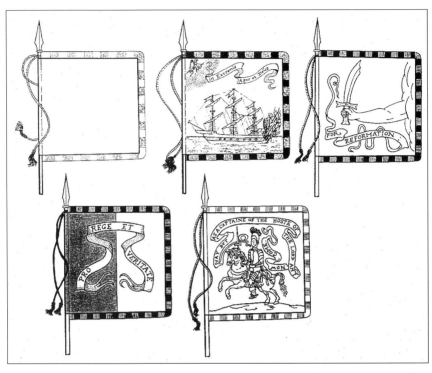

Parliamentarian cavalry 'cornets': top left, Cromwell's white flag; top centre, with ship motif, Rawlinson's troop of Dodding's Lancashire regiment; top right, unidentified; bottom left, Lambert's, with red and blue ground; bottom right, Copley's.

Infantry

Nominal Strength

Fairfax's Regiment of Foot, Colonel Sir Thomas Fairfax
(absent in the south):
Known officers: Lt Col. William Cowell, Major White,
Capt. James Priest, Capt James Pitson, Capt. Clement Keane,
Capt. George Baldwin, Capt. Charles Bolton,
Capt. William Leigh, Capt. William Farley   800
Deane's Regiment of Foot, Colonel Richard Deane:
Known officers: Capt. Henry Flower (wounded at Pembroke),
Capt. Thomas Walker, Lt Shipman   800
Pride's Regiment of Foot, Colonel Thomas Pride:
Known officers: Lt Col. William Goffe, Major Gregson
(wounded Chepstow and replaced by John Mason),
Capt. Joseph Sakill, Capt. John Hawes   800

Overton's Regiment of Foot, Colonel Robert Overton
(absent at Hull):
Known officers: Lt Col. Thomas Reade, Major Wade,
Capt. William Knowles, Capt William Gough,
Capt. Thomas Hughes, Capt. Robert Reade,
Capt. Edward Orpin. Six companies   480
Theoretical maximum   2,880

Cromwell estimated the strength of his 'horse and dragoons' at 2,500 and his
foot at 4,000, including Northern Association troops, so it is likely that the
above figures are fairly accurate. Although there were minor losses in south
Wales, the New Model had only recently had its infantry and cavalry regiment
sizes reduced to 800 and 480 men respectively, so it is probable that they were
near optimum strength. Full infantry regiments were ten companies each of
80 men, cavalry regiments six troops of 80, and dragoons were still in troops
of 100 with ten troops to a regiment.

Northern Association Army

Commander	Major General John Lambert

Nominal Strength

Lambert's Regiment of Horse:
Known officers: Lt Col. Goodrich, Major Rokeby,
Capt Baines   480
Capt. Pockly, Lt J. Hodgson, Lt. Elwand, Capt. Stoddart
Lilburne's Regiment of Horse, Colonel Robert Lilburne:
Known officers: Major Sanderson, Major Smithson,
Capt. Thomas Lilburne, Capt. Bradford, Capt Wilkinson   480
Bright's Regiment of Foot, Colonel John Bright:
Known officers: Major Pownall, Lt Hodgson   800
horse   960
foot   800

Cromwell and Lambert: combined totals

Cavalry   3,320
Infantry   3,680

Lancashire Militias

Cromwell gives the strength of the locally raised Lancashire troops as only
'about five hundred' horse and 'sixteen hundred' foot. Other contemporary

estimates vary between 2,000 and 3,000 total, with Sir James Turner favouring the larger figure.

Commander   Colonel Ashton.

Cavalry

approximate numbers

Lt Colonel Alexander Rigby's Regiment of Horse:
Known officer; Capt Rawlinson (Furness troop)   250
Colonel Nicholas Shuttleworth's Regiment of Horse   250

Infantry

Colonel Ashton's Regiment of Foot	320
Colonel Dodding's Regiment of Foot	320
Colonel Standish's Regiment of Foot	320
Colonel Rigby's Regiment of Foot	
(temporarily commanded by Standish)	320
Colonel Oughtred Shuttleworth's Regiment of Foot	320

Other known officers in the force included Major Jackson, and Captain Samuel Birch.

Total Lancashire Parliamentarians:

Cavalry	500
Infantry	1,600

Other Parliamentarian Forces

In addition to the regiments enumerated above there were a limited number of other parliamentarian forces in the north west theatre of war; as for example the county militia of Cheshire, which under Colonel Duckenfield, would raise three foot regiments, Lothian's, Croxton's, and Massey's, each of 600 men. Derbyshire and Staffordshire would similarly raise troops which would play a minor role in the latter part of the campaign. Very few of these troops would have any influence on the battle of Preston on 17 August, or the fight at Winwick. A certain number were however within one or two days march of Preston and were involved after 17 August, and should, for the sake of completeness, be mentioned:

Lancaster Garrison unlikely to number more than	500
Lascelles' Regiment	800
Wastal's Regiment	800

Lascelles was listed as a Lt Colonel under Lambert in the Northern Association army of 1647–48. Cromwell lists both Lascelles' and Wastal's as being left in Preston on 20 August 1648, but does not enumerate them in any account of the battle. Very probably one of these units was that with the 'black colours' from Durham; state papers correspondence suggests that they were under control of the committee at York. It is surmised that they would have been equal in strength to the New Model regiments. Benson's and Brigg's militia regiments from Kendal and Barrow respectively monitered the Scottish progress in July 1648 but do not appear to have played any further part in the proceedings.

Other Parliamentarian Troops approx. 2,100

Grand total Parliamentarian forces, Lancashire theatre of war, 17 August 1648

Cavalry	3,820
Infantry	7,380
Guns	Fortress only
Grand total (approximate)	11,200

Appendix II

Pay Lists

List of Pay as Promulgated 10 December 1647, by General Lambert for the Army of the Parliamentarian Northern Association. (York Minster Library, Mss, BB 53)

The Foot

Each Foote Souldier 6d. a day
Gentleman of armes 7d. a day
Corporall of foote 7d. a day
Drummer 7d. a day
Sergeant 9d. a day
Drum Major 9d. a day

Each Quarter Master 3s. 6d. a day
Ensign 2s. 4d. a day
Lieutenant 3s. a day
Captain Lieutenant 3s. 6d. a day
Captain 5s. a day
Major 6s. 6d. a day
Lt Colonel 7s. a day
Colonel 8s. a day

The Horse

Each Trooper, mounted 1s. 6d. a day
Trooper, unmounted 9d. a day
Trumpeter, Corporall 1s. 8d. a day
Chyrurgeons mate 1s. 8d. a day

Quartermaster 4s. a day
Cornet 5s. a day
Lieutenant 6s. a day
Captain Lieutenant 7s. a day
Captain 8s. a day
Major 8s. 6d. a day
Colonel 9s.

Dragoons

Each Dragoon, mounted 1s. a day
Dragoon unmounted 7d. a day
Corporall, drummer 1s. 6d. a day
Sergeant 1s. 7d. a day

Quartermaster 3s. 4d. a day
Cornet 4s. a day
Lieutenant 4s. 6d. a day
Captain 5s. 6d. a day

Artillery and Staff

Each Gunners Mate 1s. a day   Each Chaplaine 5s. a day

Common Gunner 10d. a day   Chyurgeon 4s. a day

Each Matross 8d. a day   Deputy muster master 3s. a day

Chief Gunner 2s. a day   Joynt Commissary of the musters 3s. 6d.

Marshall's man (seven) 1s. 8d.   Marshall General Lieutenant 3s. a day

Marshall General 4s. 6d. a day

Judge advocate and Council secretary 7s.

Muster master General 7s. a day

Scoutmaster General 12s. a day

Chyrurgeon General 7s. a day

(All ranks were to find their own quarters if in receipt of these sums)

List of pay for the Lancashire Militia as recorded by Samuel Birch for his infantry company.

Captain 7s 6d a day

Lieutenant 4s a day

Ensign 3s a day

Sergeant 1s 6d a day

Drummer 1s a day

Corporal 1s a day

Foot soldier 8d a day

Appendix III

The Prisoners

Three major lists of the captured survive, though as was usual at this period only the officers, and in certain cases non commissioned officers, were thought worthy of listing by name. One list contained in the pamphlet *A Great Victory At Appleby* gives the names of English Royalists taken by Colonel Ashton after the surrender of Appleby Castle. Another list, of Scottish prisoners, forms an appendix to the pamphlet *Three Letters Concerning the Surrender of Many Scottish Lords*. The last list, of *Officers Taken at Uttoxeter* was originally printed with an account of the surrender at Colchester. Most other listings are not as complete, or appear to be derivative from these documents. A collection of named individuals from other sources is at the end of this section.

Royalists taken at Appleby, 9 October 1648

Colonel Sir Philip Musgrave
Colonel Sir Robert Strickland
Colonel Sir Thomas Dacres
Colonel William Middleton
Colonel Henry Wogan
Colonel Edward Gerhard
Colonel Richard Egerton
Colonel Gerhard Lowther

Colonel Sir Thomas Tyldesley
Colonel Sir William Huddleston
Colonel Sir Philip Blackstone
Colonel Henry Chester
Colonel William Carleton
Colonel George Denton
Colonel Edward Chesnall

Lt Col. Roscarick (Governor of Appleby)
Lt Col. Phillipson
Lt Col. Ewbanke
Lt Col. Crackenthorpe
Lt Col. Corney

Lt Col. Edward Hutchinson
Lt Col. Bellingham
Lt Col. Strickland
Lt Col. Holt
Lt Col. Corney

Serg. Major Thomas Glasier
Serg. Major William Hodgkinson
Serg. Major James Butler

Serg. Major Michael Moone
Serg. Major Thmas Sandys
Serg. Major William Wandell

Capt. Henry Musgrave

Capt. John Denton

Capt. Robert Hilton
Capt. William Musgrave
Capt. John Thompson
Capt. Henry Brabin
Capt. Edward Wright
Capt. John Dracott
Capt. Samuel Potter
Capt. John Harling
Capt. Robert Dixon
Capt. John Croft
Capt. Robert Wormley
Capt. Thomas Sandford
Capt. John Bamfield
Capt. Samuel Beale
Capt. Francis Wood
Capt. Thomas Leigh
Capt Edward Lamplugh
Capt. John Stevenson
Capt. Launcelot Walker
Capt. Edward Worley
Capt. Henry Ashton
Capt. Moone

Capt. John Hilton
Capt. Richard Baxter
Capt. Homer
Capt. Robert Westley
Capt. Rowland Beckingham
Capt. Edward Revell
Capt. John Bickley
Capt. Peter Shepperd
Capt. Humphrey Bagguly
Capt. Henry Crossland
Capt. Page
Capt. Ralph Willie
Capt. Richard Lowther
Capt. Philip Catroni
Capt. Michael Lyme
Capt. Stephen Page
Capt. John Whelpdale
Capt. Robert Leake
Capt. Thomas Maxfield
Capt. Robert Highington
Capt. George Hudson
Capt. William Hardcot

Lt William Huddleston
Lt Bayley
Lt Philip Dracot
Lt John Osbaderson
Lt Robert Moon
Lt Crackenthorp
Lt John Hodgiton
Lt Danking
Lt Patrick Hamilton

Lt Richard Barker
Lt Wilfrid Carey
Lt John Whiteside
Lt John Sergeant
Lt Henry Banks
Lt Robert Long
Lt Christopher Rawley
Lt Bartholemew Hough

Cornet Daniel Mayes
Cornet Richard Harford
Cornet William Curtis
Cornet Henry Lampleigh
Cornet Thomas Bowyer

Cornet John Barchel
Cornet William Richardson
Cornet John Cholmley
Cornet Richard Staindy
Cornet William Blencesset

Ensign Henry Harling
Ensign John Peacock

Ensign Henry Sewell

Officers of the train
Richard Walker
John Singleton

Judge Advocate
Edward Constable

Chaplains
Francis Gest
Mr Young

Doctor
Samuel Stephens

Other ranks: in excess of 1,000

Scottish Prisoners taken from Baillie's Command Warrington, 19 August 1648

Argyle's Regiment

Capt. Daniel Campbell
Lt Patrick Campbell
Lt John Menzies
Lt William Musgrave
Lt Hugh Mackellar

Lt Patrick Mackara
Lt Thomas Buchannan
Lt Alexander Campbell
Lt Patrick Hemant
Lt John Stewart

Other ranks: 5 Sergeants

General of the Artillery's Regiment

Major Hamilton
Capt. Engham
Other ranks: 5 Sergeants, 46 Privates

Lt Murray

Earl of Atholl's Regiment

Lt Col. William Ogilvy

Capt. Robert Stewart
Ensign Belsay
Ensign William Sandbyn
Ensign Thomas Ewing

Ensign James Jackson
Ensign Patrick Blair
Ensign Henry Stelbart
Ensign John Robinson

Other ranks: 5 Sergeants, 155 private soldiers

Lt General Baillie's Regiment

Lt General William Baillie
Major Walter Scott   Capt. James Baillie
Ensign Patrick Home   Ensign Robert Johnson

Other ranks: 4 Sergeants, 120 private soldiers

Lord Bargany's Regiment

Major James Somerville   Capt. John Veitch
Lt Alexander Tweedie   Lt Robert Hamilton
Ensign William Veitch (or Peach)   Ensign George Bruce

Other ranks: 4 Sergeants, 80 private soldiers

Lord Carnegie's Regiment

Col. James Lord Carnegie

Lt Col. William Hamilton
Capt Richardson   Lt Robert Dundas
Lt Archibald Linsay   Lt James Wilson
Lt James Forbes   Lt Alexander Caddle

Ensign David Carnegie   Ensign John Crishen
Ensign James Sinclair   Ensign John Garden
Ensign William Mumtor

Other ranks: 8 Sergeants, 140 private soldiers

Colonel Richard Douglas' Regiment

Colonel Douglas

Major William Douglas   Ensign Andrew Scot
Ensign William Scot   Ensign Archibald Scot
Ensign William Rutherford   Ensign Robert Douglas
Ensign James Scot   Ensign James Harleton
Ensign Alexander Pringle   Ensign William Rutherford

Other ranks: 7 Sergeants, 124 private soldiers

Sir James Drummond of Machanie's Regiment

Major Alexander Fleming

Lt John Drummond   Capt. William Drummond
Lt Walter Mackenell   Ensign William Hamble
Ensign William Drummond   Ensign William Drummond
Ensign John Davis   Ensign John Burdine

Other ranks: 2 Sergeants, 90 Private soldiers

Earl of Dumfries' Regiment

Lt Col. John Johnston(e)

Capt. William Johnston   Lt Patrick Johnston
Lt John Crichton   Lt Patrick Johnston
Lt George Murray   Lt John Johnston
Ensign James Johnston

Other ranks: 4 Sergeants, 44 private soldiers

Sir Alexander Fraser of Philorth's Firelocks

Capt. John Fraser   Capt. Leslie

Lt James Reade   Lt William Faulconer
Ensign James Leslie   Ensign Johnson

Other ranks: 4 Sergeants, 150 private soldiers

Sir John Grey's Regiment

Ensign James Fergusson   Ensign James Abercrombie
Quartermaster Alexander Gibson

Other ranks: 2 Sergeants, 32 private soldiers

Duke of Hamilton's Regiment

Sergeant Major Baillie   Capt. Hugh Marwell
Capt. Gabriel Hamilton   Capt. Archibald Hamilton
Capt. George Hamilton   Capt. Baillie

Capt. James Hamilton
Lt John Hamilton

Lt Francis Baillie
Lt John Cormick

Ensign David Forsyth
Ensign David Lindsay
Ensign James Inglis

Ensign David Scot
Ensign Francis Hamilton

Other ranks: 19 Sergeants, 360 private soldiers

Lord Home's Regiment

Lt Col. Alexander Home

Capt. Lt Peter Home
Lt Glendinning
Lt Home
Ensign Robert Watson
Ensign Moir
Ensign Browne

Lt William Dickson
Lt Kerr
Ensign David Home
Ensign Rollo
Ensign Merchison

Other ranks: 14 Sergeants, 250 Private soldiers

Colonel George Keith's Regiment

Capt. Lt John Greig
Lt Patrick Blair
Ensign Robert Grahame
Ensign James Atkins

Lt James Keith
Ensign James Keith
Ensign Andrew Leslie
Ensign Alexander Keith

Other ranks: 4 sergeants, 130 private soldiers

Earl of Kellie's Regiment

Lt Robert Lindsay
Ensign John Dickson
Ensign John Pearson

Ensign Thomas Hamilton
Ensign Peter Borthill

Other ranks: 5 Sergeants, 100 private soldiers

Colonel Harry Maule's Regiment

Col. Henry, or Harry, Maule (captured but later escaped)

Lt Andrew Wood   Ensign Robert Lisbine
Ensign Alexander Duguid   Ensign James Gentleman
Quartermaster Robert Irvine

Other ranks: 3 Sergeants, 119 private soldiers

Earl of Roxburgh's Regiment

Lt Col. Andrew Kerr (probably, since he signed Baillie's apologia)

Lt James Campbell   Ensign William Rutherford
Quartermaster Alexander Latie

Other ranks: 3 Sergeants, 30 private soldiers

Earl of Tullibardine's Regiment

Major John Fleming   Lt David Hitton
Lt Andrew Napper   Ensign James Campbell

Other ranks: 11 Sergeants, 116 private soldiers

Colonel James Turner's Regiment

Lt Col. George Meldrum

Major Malcolm Somerville   Ensign Andrew Rottsome
Ensign Andrew Ogilvy   Ensign Nicholas Browne

Other ranks: 7 Sergeants, 120 private soldiers

John Hay, Master of Yester's Regiment

Capt. Thomas Hamilton   Capt. Alexander Auchmuty
Capt. Edmond Hay   Lt Graham
Lt Abercrombie   Lt Tweedie
Lt Hume   Lt Strudsham
Lt Clerke   Lt Ungton
Lt Weir   Lt Houston
Lt Humes   Lt Cochrane
Lt Taite   Lt Cranston
Lt Hay   Lt Murrey
Lt William Cranston

Other ranks: 12 Sergeants, 50 private soldiers
Total number of prisoners taken at Warrington
as given in original document   2,547

Prisoners taken at Uttoxeter

The Duke of Hamilton

Col. Bargany (Lord John Bargeny)
Col. Mills   Lt Col. Dalmaboy
Col. Carr   Lt Col. Ogleag
Col. Ramsay (George Lord Ramsay)   Lt Col. Blayre
Col. Blayre   Lt Col. Cooper
Col. Lockhead   Lt Col. Drummond
Col. Fowles (Sir James Foules)   Lt Col. Dicke
Col. Turner (adjutant Gen)   Lt Col. Hamilton

Maj. James Boswell   Maj. George Simpson
Maj. Crawford   Maj. Crooks
Maj. Sharpe   Maj. Hamilton
Maj. Ennis (Quarter Master Innis?) Maj. Middleton
Maj. Wood   Maj. Deands
Maj. Gibb   Maj. Carre
Maj. Lickwood

Capt. White   Capt. St Clare   Capt. Dalmaboy
Capt. Strachen   Capt. Liseley   Capt. Hay
Capt. Camben   Capt. Stretton   Capt. Middleton
Capt. Mayneyes   Capt. Albert   Capt. Alex. Hamilton
Capt. Somerell   Capt. Blaire   Capt. Tompson
Capt. Robertson   Capt. Pringle   Capt. Rutherford
Capt. Monoeroth   Capt. Levingstone   Capt. Will. Hoith
Capt. Cunningham   Capt. Maxwell   Capt. Mongomery
Capt. Smith   Capt. Borthwicke   Capt. Scot
Capt. Joyce   Capt. Rives   Capt. Douglas

Lt Strechard   Lt Libertan   Lt Junis
Lt Douglas   Lt Bleive   Lt Ramsey
Lt Fauks   Lt Sinclare   Lt Jo. Stroud
Lt Munhead   Lt Hamilton   Lt Gibb
Lt Rosse   Lt Jo. Graham   Lt Murry

Lt Hunter

Lt Cleaveland

Lt Bulley

Lt Knox

Lt Tumbrill

Lt O'Neale

Lt O'Lauget

Lt Callender

Lt Gavin Hamilton

Lt Drummond

Lt Stewart

Lt Innis

Lt Bunchay

Lt Menteith

Lt Primrose

Lt Barkley

Lt Burnsed

Lt Garmond

Lt Dyun

Lt Jo. Hamilton

Lt Johnstone

Lt Lodi Hamilton

Lt Humbruton

Lt Abernethy

Lt Mayre

Cornet Kauk

Cornet Blayre

Cornet Grahum

Cornet Reade

Cornet Hunter

Cornet Gibbald

Cornet Skernam

Cornet Hay

Cornet Meldram

Cornet Bell

Cornet Crichton

Cornet Levingstone

Cornet Hay

Cornet Hamilton

Cornet Steward

Cornet Cambells

Cornet Treasure

Cornet Hamilton

Cornet Edmiston

Cornet Spint

Cornet Bell

Quarter Masters:

Blackley

Oswell

St Hell

Barnes

Sampson

Kyneere

Johnston

Levingstone

Laky

Wilston

Browne

Gaston

Horne

Cumbell

Heath

Dunbarr

Clegorne

Hamilton

Vaux

Cambell

Corporals:

Carr

Levingstone

Crighton

Monroe

Kelley

Morchell

Edom

Mer

Newton

Teate

Wilson

Wilson

Gray

Matland

Tald

Douglas

Kevaday

Duffe

Douglas

Dunstaine

Hunter

Hebron

More

Barkley

Anderson

Lockheart

Craford

Mungumre

Wilson

Bathano

Fouler

Cider

Hunter

Trumpeters:

John Whit	James Ramsell	John Mackey
Walter Jackson	John Wright	

Duke of Hamilton's servants:

Mr Cole	Mr James Hamilton	Mr Lewis
Mr Jo. Hamilton	Mr Robert Hamilton	Mr James Skene
Thomas Hamilton	Patrick Hamilton	Walter Whitson
John Clark	James Taylor	William Jack
John Tench	Wil. Hamilton	Robert Hamilton
Ralph Richinson	James Bishop	Francis Brown
Valentine Baldwin	Jo. Bell	Alexander Simpson
George Pitman	Robert Robson	Nathaniel Peierson
James Hamilton	Cornelius Herne	David Coulte
Thomas Wilson	Archibald Hamilton	Will. Bleakbunn
Thomas Miller	William Gilmore	William Strong
Mr Standidge	Mr Joh. Herbert	Robert Flemming
John Lenrick	Rich. Sterenton	John Flemming
William Tompson	James Patterson	Robert Nesmoth
John Allen	John Johnson	James Douglas
Henry Wickson	Alexander Fite	William Monerherd
John Buggan	Tho. Mudell	William Fountain
Andrew Hinsburne	William Menerherd	David Cunningham
John Hunter	David Honind	John Browne
Jowen Hamilton	David Bisset	John Edgar
James Dynn	William Keimance	

(these 'servants' may perhaps have been gentleman volunteers, and survivors of Hamilton's Lifeguard rather than simply menials in the modern sense.)

'Common Souldiers Neer Upon 3000.'

Other prisoners known to have been taken at Preston, Nantwich, Nottingham, and elsewhere not already listed

General Sir Marmaduke Langdale
Lieutenant General, James Earl of Callander
Lieutenant General, John Middleton
Sir James Lesley
Sir Michael Mishmish
Lord Lunton
Colonel William, Lord Cranston

Drummer.   *Fifer.*

Nineteenth-century copies of seventeenth-century illustrations of a fifer and
drummer: the two most usual instruments to be found in an infantry regiment.

Colonel Sir Lewis Dives
Colonel Galliard
Colonel Claudius (or Claude) Hamilton
Colonel George Keith
Colonel William Owen
Colonel John Earl of Traquair
Colonel John Urry
Colonel William Urry
Colonel Vandruske
Major Constable
Capt. Thomas Meldrum
Other ranks: perhaps 3,000 at Preston itself, 100 at Wigan and various
small parties from Cheshire, the Ribble Valley, Cumberland and elsewhere.

Total number of Royalist and Scottish prisoners in excess of 11,000.

Notes

1. Battle in 1648

1. The late Brigadier P. Young has written extensively on battles of the first Civil War: see for example *Edgehill*, Kineton (1967); *Naseby*, London (1985); and *The Cavalier Army* (1974). Ian Roy's *Royalist Ordnance Papers* (Oxfordshire Record Society, 1964 and 1976) is also useful, as is R. Hutton, *The Royalist War Effort* (1982). Handy introductions are provided by K. Roberts, *Soldiers of the Civil War: Infantry* (1989), and J. Tincey, *Soldiers of the Civil War: Cavalry* (1990). C. H. Firth, *Cromwell's Army* (1902 reprinted London, 1962) remains a classic.

2. See D. Blackmore, *Arms and Armour of the English Civil Wars* (1990), pp. 63–8, 75–81.

3. Many drill books describe this: see for example Gervase Markham, *The Soldiers Exercise* (London, 1639), pp. 2–3. The Royal Armouries and York Castle Museum both contain outstanding collections of Civil War arms and Armour.

4. Turner, *Pallas Armata* (London, 1683), pp. 168–70.

5. R. Brooke, *Visits to Battlefields of England* (1857), p. 214. On firearms development see C. Blair (ed.), *Pollard's History of Firearms* (New York, 1983), pp. 25–105, and B. P. Hughes, *Firepower* (1974), pp. 10–41, 73–5.

6. See H. Blackmore, *British Military Firearms* (1961), pp. 1–44, and his *Dictionary of London Gunmakers* (Oxford, 1986); also W. M. Stern, 'Gunmaking in seventeenth-century London', *Journal of the Arms and Armour Society*, vol. i, no. 5, 1954, pp. 55–100. John Lambert is known to have owned a copy of Barriffe's work, also the influential *Tactics of Aelian* (1616); see Dawson, pp. 425–8.

7. Roger, Earl of Orrery, *A Treatise on the Art of War* (London, 1677), p. 30.

8. See Museum of London Ms. 46–78/709; also G. I. Mungeam, 'Contracts for the supply of equipment to the New Model', *Journal of the Arms and Armour Society*, vol. vi, no. 3, 1968, pp. 53–115; R. Elton., *Compleat Body of the Art Military* (London, 1650), p. 145. Also useful is D. E. Lewis, *The Office of Ordnance and the Parliamentarian Land Forces 1642–1648*, unpublished PhD thesis, Loughborough University, 1976, *passim*.

9. W. Barriffe, *Militarie Discipline or the Young Artilleryman* (London, 1661), pp. 171–3; G. Parker, *The Military Revolution* (Cambridge, 1988), pp. 19–24; B. Nosworthy, *The Anatomy of Victory* (New York, 1990), pp. 1–52. See also S. Reid, 'Scots Infantry in the 1640s', *Military Illustrated*, no. 19, July 1989, pp. 27–32.

10. A very useful book for civil war cavalry is J. Cruso, *Militarie Instructions for the Cavalrie* (reprinted with an introduction by P. Young, Kineton, 1972); also important is J. Vernon, *The Young Horseman* (London, 1644).

11. A good deal of data on cavalry equipment is contained in P.R.O. WO 47/1–2; and in D. E. Lewis, *op cit*.

12. See D. Blackmore, *op cit*, pp. 24–44, also A. G. Credland 'Some swords of the English Civil War', *Journal of the Arms and Armour Society*, vol, x no. 6, 1982, pp. 196–205.

13. See S. B. Bull, *The Furie of the Ordnance*, unpublished PhD thesis, University of Wales, Swansea, 1988, *passim*; also D. Stevenson and D. H. Caldwell, 'Leather guns and other light artillery in seventeenth-century Scotland', *Proceedings of the Society of Antiquaries of Scotland*, 1976–7, pp. 300–17.

14. W. Money, *The First and Second Battles of Newbury* (1884), p. 161; *A True Relation of the Diurnal Marchings of the Red and Blew Regiments of the Trained Bands of the City of London* (London, 1643), *passim*; 'MZB', 'The Battle of Newburn' (Glasgow, 1643, reprinted in *Fugitive Scottish Poetry*, Edinburgh, 1853).

2. Forces

1. See M. Kishlansky, *The Rise of the New Model Army* (New York, 1979). Also I. Gentles, *The New Model Army* (Oxford, 1992), pp. 1–53, and D. E. Lewis, *The Office of Ordnance and the Parliamentarian Land Forces*, unpublished PhD thesis, Loughborough, 1976.

2. Gentles, pp. 16–25; J. Sprigge, *Anglia Rediviva* (London, 1647), pp. 7–52, 325–35.

3. *Regimental History*, pp. xiii-xxi; S. Bull, *Fury of the Ordnance*, p. 408, n. 433.

4. D.N.B., Harrison, Sexby; *Regimental History*, pp. 163–75. On Cromwell see W. C. Abbott, *A Bibliography of Oliver Cromwell* (Harvard, 1929).

5. L. Hutchinson, *Memoirs of Colonel Hutchinson* (1846), pp. 49, 136, 320, 322; *Regimental History*, pp. 264–77.

6. D.N.B., Okey, Deane, Pride, Bright; *Regimental History*, pp. 291–307, 317–36, 346–59, 404–17.

7. *Regimental History*, pp. 253–67; Dawson, pp. 28–66. See also P. Gwilliam, *The Political and Military Career of General John Lambert*, unpublished MPhil, University of Leeds, 1988.

8. L. Boynton, *The Elizabethan Militia 1558–1638* (1967), pp. 13–50, 244–397.

9. Ormerod, pp. 250–51; Broxap, p. 160.

10. Hodgson, pp. 118–19.

11. D.N.B., Hamilton. See also D. Stevenson, *The Scottish Revolution 1637–1644* (Edinburgh, 1973).

12. Burnet, p. 449.

13. D.N.B., Turner; Turner, pp. 3–50.

14. Carlyle, p. 294; Burnet, p. 451; Dawson, p. 70.

15. Ormerod, p. 254.

16. E. M. Furgol, *A Regimental History of the Covenanting Armies* (Edinburgh, 1990), pp. 268–91; S. Reid, *The Scots Armies of the Seventeenth Century*, in four parts (Leigh-on-Sea, *c*.1985–1990); S. Reid 'Covenanters: Scots infantry in the 1640s', *Military Illustrated*, no. 19, June 1989, pp. 27–32.

17. Turner, pp. 50–9.

18. Furgol, *op cit.*, pp. 285–6; Turner p. 44; Burnet, pp. 442, 452–3. See also D. Stevenson, *Scottish Covenanters and Irish Confederates* (Belfast 1981), pp. 253–68.

19. Newman, pp. 221–3; D.N.B., Langdale; F. H. Sunderland, *Marmaduke Lord Langdale* (1926).

20. Musgrave, p. 304.
21. Newman, p. 167.
22. Musgrave, pp. 303–4; Reade, pp. 293–4.

3. The Coming of the Second Civil War

1. The literature on the first civil war is more extensive than that of the second. Well worth consulting on the aspects mentioned here are: C. Russell, *The Causes of the English Civil War* (Oxford, 1990); H. Tomlinson (ed.), *Before the English Civil War* (Basingstoke, 1983); R. Ashton, *The English Civil War* (1978); C. V. Wedgewood, *The King's War* (1958); P. Newman, *The Battle of Marston Moor* (Chichester, 1981); P. Young, *Marston Moor 1644* (Kineton, 1970); M. Ashley, *Naseby* (Stroud, 1992); R. Hutton, *The Royalist War Effort* (1982); J. Kenyon, *The Civil Wars of England* (1988); J. Morrill (ed.), *Reactions to the English Civil War* (1982). Much older, but useful, are the classic *History of the Rebellion by Clarendon*, edited by W. D Macray (1888), and S. R. Gardiner, *History of the Great Civil War* (1891–1893). On the Lancashire situation see B. G. Blackwood, 'Parties and issues in the Civil War in Lancashire', *Transactions of the Historic Society of Lancashire and Cheshire*, vol. cxxxii, Essays Presented to J. J. Bagley, 1983, pp. 103–26.
2. Order Book of the Council of the Northern Parliamentary Army, York Minster Library, BB 53, ff 1–23. The pay list is reproduced as Appendix II.
3. One of the best anthologies of 'Leveller' thought is A. L. Morton (ed.), *Freedom in Arms* (1975), which also has a useful introduction. See also H. Trevor-Roper (ed.), *Selections from Clarendon* (Oxford, 1978), pp. 281–95, and J. Morrill, *The Revolt of the Provinces* (1976), pp. 125–31, 203–8.
4. See J. D. Jones, *The Royal Prisoner* (1965), pp. 19–97; F. Bamford, *A Royalist's Notebook: The Commonplace Book of Sir John Oglander* (1936), pp. 111–22; P. Gregg, *King Charles I* (1981), pp. 405–31; C. Carlton, *Charles I* (1983), pp. 305–19.
5. D. Stevenson, *Scottish Covenanters and Irish Confederates* (Belfast, 1981), p. 254.
6. Carlyle, p. 269; P. Gaunt, *A Nation Under Siege* (1991), pp. 65–73. On north Wales see N. Tucker, *North Wales in the Civil War* (1958, reprinted Wrexham, 1992), pp. 131–64.
7. H. F. Abell, *Kent and the Great Civil War* (Ashford, 1901), pp. 167–205; J. Wilson, *Fairfax* (New York, 1985), pp. 95–141; Woolrych, pp. 153–65.

4. The Northern Campaign. April to August 1648

1. Sunderland, pp. 111–14.
2. Musgrave, pp. 304–6; B.L., E 448 (7).
3. Hamilton, pp. 182–97.
4. H.M.C. Thirteenth Report, Appendix, part 1; *Manuscripts of the Duke of Portland*, vol. 1 (1891), p. 455, letter from Stockdale to Thorp; Sanderson, pp. 18–20; C.S.P.D., vol. dxvi, pp. 130, 136–7.
5. Hamilton, p. 210; C.S.P.D., vol. dxvi, p. 130.
6. Birch, pp. 173–4.
7. Hamilton, pp. 217–27; Reade, p. 229.
8. Sanderson, pp. 19–20; Dawson, pp. 68–72; B.L., E 446 (12).

9. Birch, p. 175; Dawson, pp. 72–8; B.L., E 454 (10).
10. Carlyle, p. 274; Hodgson, pp. 106–12.
11. C.S.P.D., vol. i, p. 210.
12. *Memoirs of Colonel Hutchinson*, pp. 316–19; C.S.P.D., vol. dxvi, p. 230.
13. Burnet, pp. 453–4.
14. Langdale, p. 2.
15. *Discourse*, p. 65; Turner, p. 62; Carlyle, p. 289; Sanderson, p. 20.
16. Birch, p. 175.

5. 'Bloudy Preston'

1. Hodgson, pp. 115–16; Carlyle, pp. 282–3; Langdale, pp. 2–3; *Moderate Intelligencer*, B.L., B 58/84 (72).
2. The old Guildhall edifice collapsed ignominiously at 6 a.m. on Saturday 3 June 1780, the morning after a ball was held there.
3. See John Taylor (ed.), *A Brief Description of the Borough and Town of Preston . . . Originally Composed Between The Years 1682 and 1686* (Preston, 1818). Watery Lane can be found either by turning right off Fishwick View just before Tamar Street, near the junction with Arnhem Road, or alternately by following the track which passes the Shaws Arms public house.
4. Hodgson, p. 117.
5. Burnet, p. 454.
6. *Discourse*, p. 65.
7. L.R.O., DDX 194/28. Eighteenth-century estate maps also give some impression, but the enclosed and built-up areas expanded rapidly during the latter part of that century.
8. Hodgson, p. 118; *Moderate Intelligencer*, B.L., B 58/84 (72).
9. J. Walton's letter in *The Bloudy Battle at Preston in Lancashire, 1648*.
10. Carlyle, p. 291.
11. Turner, p. 63–4.
12. Burnet, p. 456; Turner, p. 64. Cattermole's well known painting of the battle, now at the Harris Museum, depicts approximately this point in the action and, although it telescopes events and space slightly, Hamilton's party is depicted in the water.
13. Turner, p. 64.
14. Milton, 'Ode to Cromwell'. See also Charles Hardwick, *Antient Battlefields in Lancashire* (Manchester 1882), pp. 217–18.
15. Carlyle, pp. 282–3.
16. Turner, p. 65; Burnet, p. 457.

6. Last Stand

1. Hodgson pp. 120–1; *Moderate Intelligencer*, B.L., B 58/84 (72); *Discourse*, pp. 65–6.
2. Carlyle, pp. 291–2; Hodgson, p. 121; Saunderson, pp. 20–1.
3. *Bloudy Battel at Preston, 1648. A Copy of Lieutenant General Crumwels Letter, Read in the House of Commons, and other Letters Of a great and Bloody Fight Neere Preston* (London, 1648); Birch, pp. 173–86. See also *The Overthrow of the Scottish Army or a Letter from Lieutenant General Cromwell to the Committee of Lancashire* (London, 1648).
4. Carlyle, pp. 292–3. See also L.R.O., DP 223, Lieutenant General Cromwell's Letter;

Turner, pp. 65–8; Burnet, p. 457; H. Wardale, 'Cromwell in Lancashire', *Transactions of the Lancashire and Cheshire Antiquarian Society*, vol. xlviii, 1934, pp. 76–93; C. Carlton, *Going to the Wars* (1992), pp. 324–7.

5. Burnet, p. 458; Hodgson, p. 123. See also G. Ashby, 'Winwick Pass', in *Civil War Notes and Queries*, xiii, pp. 2–4.

6. *Discourse*, p. 66; *Moderate Intelligencer*, B.L., B 58/84 (72). Carlyle, p. 293.

7. Baillie, pp. 456–7; Broxap, pp. 168–71; Woolrych, pp. 175–84.

8. See S. Reid, *Scots Colours* (Leigh-on-Sea, 1990); also *Three Letters Concerning The Surrender of Many Scottish Lords to the High Sherriff of the County of Chester* (London 1648). Some doubt exists about 'Major' Cholmley's rank, and in any case more than one member of the family was serving: see Dawson, pp. 79–80.

9. Turner, pp. 68–74; Sanderson, p. 21; C.S.P.D. vol. dxvi, p. 136; Burnet, pp. 460–2; Musgrave, p. 307; Clarke Mss., vol 70, f131. On the Cheshire militia see R. N. Dore, *The Civil Wars in Cheshire* (Chester, 1966), pp. 71–2.

10. *Colchester surrendered to the Lord General, also a list of Officers taken with the Duke Hambleton at Uttoxeter, 25 August by the Lord Grey*, B.L., E 461 (15); S.R.O., Quarter Sessions Papers, cited in G. Joiner, *Staffordshire in the Civil War* (Staffordshire County Council, 1993), p. 34.

11. Sunderland, pp. 131–45; Hutchinson, pp. 324–5.

7. Results

1. H. F. Abell, *Kent and the Great Civil War* (Ashford, 1901), pp. 167–250; M. Carter, *A True Relation of that unfortunate Expedition of Kent, Essex and Colchester, 1648* (1650); D. Woodward and C. Cockerill, *The Siege of Colchester, 1648: a History and Bibliography* (Essex Libraries, 1979); Woolrych, pp. 182–4.

2. C.S.P.D., vol. dxvi, p. 256. On captured colours see Fisher B.L. Harl. Manuscript 1460.

3. C.W.T., *A Great Victory at Appleby* (London, 1648), also reprinted in Ormerod, pp. 273–4; Musgrave, pp. 310–11.

4. Burnet, pp. 463–500.

5. J. D. Jones, *The Royal Prisoner*, pp. 108–38; Woolrych, *Battles of the Civil War*, pp. 179–84; C. Carlton, *Charles I* (1983), pp. 320–60; P. Gregg, *King Charles I* (1981), pp. 404–49.

6. Although published as though written by the king, *Eikon Basiliske* was probably penned by John Gauden, the Dean of Bocking, in Essex. Whoever the author, it soon ran to many editions and was the start of the literature which identified Charles as a martyr. The earliest editions are dated 1648, since years were at that time run from April to April like the modern financial year. See pp. 252–69.

7. C. V. Wedgwood, *The Trial of Charles I* (1964); A. Woolrych, *England without a King* (1983); R. Ashton, 'From Cavalier to Roundhead Tyranny', in J. Morrill (ed.), *Reactions to the English Civil War* (1982), pp. 185–207; J. Wilson, *Fairfax*, pp. 123–53; Gentles, p. 260

8. Sanderson, p. 15.

9. Burnet, p. 463. See also R. Ashton, *The English Civil War* (1978), pp. 318–22.

10. See R. Holmes, *Preston 1648*, p. 46, and *Worcester 1651*.

11. J. Turner, *Pallas Armata* (London, 1683), pp. 160–2, 168–70, 174, 178–86, 260–62: S. Anglo, *Machiavelli: A Dissection* (1969), pp. 129–57; C. H. Firth, *Cromwell's Army* (Oxford, 1911), p. 98.

12. Sunderland, pp. 150–250.

13. See T. Skinner, *The Life of General Monk* (London, 1724); W. S. Douglas, *Cromwell's Scotch Campaigns* (1899); R. Hutton, *Charles II* (Oxford, 1989), pp. 170–2; Dawson, pp. 250–457.

14. *Discourse*, p. 67; C. Carleton, *Going to the Wars* (1992), p. 327; Dawson, p. 78.

15. The Lancashire Quarter Sessions Papers provide several good examples of the deprivations occassioned by the wars. Taylor's ox is mentioned in L.R.O., QSP 10/2 (1648); others regarding widows, Scottish plunder and illegitimate children include QSP 1/6; 15/7; 9/1; 21/7; 22/18; 23/30; and 23/41.

16. Ormerod, pp. 277–9.

17. Blackwood, *Lancashire Gentry and the Great Rebellion* (Chetham Society, Manchester, 1978), pp. 111–62; L.R.O., QSP 24/27.

Bibliography

Baillie: D. Laing (ed.), *The Letters and Journals of Robert Baillie*, 3 vols (Edinburgh, 1841).

Birch: *Diary of Samuel Birch*, reprinted in Historical Manuscripts Commission, Fourteenth Report, Appendix Part II, *The Mauscripts of his Grace the Duke of Portland*, vol. 3 (London, 1894).

B.L.: British Library. References elsewhere in the notes commencing 'E' are contemporary newspapers in the Thomason Tracts collection.

Broxap: Broxap, E., *The Great Civil War in Lancashire* (Manchester, 1910).

Burnet: Burnet, G., *The Memoirs of the Lives and Actions of James and William, Dukes of Hamilton* (Oxford, 1852).

Carlyle: Carlyle, T., *Oliver Cromwell's Letters and Speeches*, 3 vols (London, 1866).

C.S.P.D.: Hamilton, W. D. (ed.), *Calendar of State Papers, Domestic Series, of the Reign of Charles I . . . Preserved in Her Majesty's Public Record Office* (London, 1893).

Dawson: *Cromwell's Understudy: The Life and Times of General John Lambert* (London, 1938).

Discourse: Beaumont, W. (ed.), *A Discourse of the Warre in Lancashire* (Chetham Society, 1864).

D.N.B.: *Dictionary of National Biography*

Gentles: Gentles, I., *The New Model Army* (Oxford, 1992).

Hamilton: Gardiner, S. R. (ed.), *The Hamilton Papers* (Camden Society, 1880).

Hodgson: *Original Memoirs Written During the Great Civil War Being the Life of Sir Henry Slingsby, and the Memoirs of Capt. Hodgson* (reprinted Edinburgh, 1806).

Holmes: Holmes, R., *Preston 1648*, British Battlefields series (Market Drayton, 1985).

Langdale: Langdale, M., *An Impartiall Relation of the Late Fight at Preston, 1648*.

L.R.O.: Lancashire Record Office (see notes)

Musgrave: Clarendon Ms. 2867, reprinted in *Miscellany of Scottish History*, vol. 2 (Edinburgh, 1904), pp. 302–11.

Newman: Newman P. *Royalist Officers* (New York, 1981).

Ormerod: Ormerod, G. (ed.), *Tracts Relating to the Military Proceedings in Lancashire During the Great Civil War* (Chetham Society, 1844). P.R.O. Public Records Office (see notes).

Reade: Clarendon Ms. 2984, reprinted in *Miscellany of Scottish History*, vol. 2 (Edinburgh, 1904), pp. 293–301.

Regimental History: Firth, C. H., *The Regimental History of Cromwell's Army* (Oxford, 1940).

Sanderson Diary: reprinted in *Proceedings of the Society of Antiquaries of Newcastle-upon-Tyne*, third series, vol. ix, 1921, pp. 8–47.

S.R.O.: Staffordshire Record Office (see notes).

Turner, Memoirs of his own Life and Times. From a manuscript dated 1670, edited by T. Thomson Bannatyne Club, 1829, and most recently reprinted, Tonbridge 1991.

Woolrych, A., *Battles of the English Civil War* (London, 1961).

Civil War Period Military Books

From the late sixteenth century there was a rapid increase in the publication of military works, both narratives of campaigns, and drill books. Together with improving standards of literacy this fact appears to have helped the develpoment of new tactics and similar, if not fully standardised, drills. Most of the relevant titles are listed in M. J. D. Cockle, *A Bibliography of Military Books up to 1642* (London, 1900, new edition 1957). In addition to these it is worth noting a few which have particular currency for the Second Civil War.

Barriffe, W., *Militarie Discipline: or the Young Artillery Man* (fourth edition, London, 1648).

Boyle, R. (Lord Orrery), *Treatise of the Art of War* (London, 1677).

Burt, N., *Militarie Instructions* (London, 1644).

Eldred, W., *The Gunner's Glasse* (London, 1646).

Elton, R., *The Compleat Body of the Art Military* (London, 1650).

Hexam, H., *Principles of the Art Militarie* (The Hague, 1637–43).

Monk, G., *Observations upon Military and Political Affairs* (London, 1671).

Norton, R., *The Gunners Dialogue* (London, 1643).

Nye, N., *The Art of Gunnery* (London, 1647).

Turner, J., *Pallas Armata* (London, 1683).

Vernon, J., *The Young Horseman* (London, 1644).

A perfect

RELATION

of

A great victory in the North, obtained by the Forces commanded by
Lieutenant Generall *Cromwell*, and Major Generall *Lambert*, against
the Scottish Forces commanded by Duke *Hamilton*, as it was certified
thence by Letter.

Sir,

 ee in these parts have suffered much by the late incursion of the
Scots, they plundering and taking away from us, all what they
saw good, sparing neither Royallist nor Presbyterian; and is any
that had acted much in their behalfe, in raising either men, money,
or been any other way their favourite, had informed the Scottish Commanders,
of what service they had done in their behalfe, and desiring that they might
be freed from plunder, and such other inconveniencies, all the answer they
could have, was this, that they conceived the best way was, for them to convey
away their goods, that it might not be a temptation to the Souldiers; for they
could not refraine them from such extravagancies: so you may see that whether
we be for them, or against them, their friends, or their enemies, all shall speed
alike; and is their friends have to better assurance to keep their goods, but the
hiding them away, they have no greater priviledge for security then their
enemies: then with what heart can any act for them? And besides their plundering of us, they lie upon free quarter, none paying for what they received,
and to augment our burthens, for many were quartered upon us, that we by
that time the Souldiers were satisfied, had not sufficient bread to put in our
mouths, and when they removed their quarters, it was because that we had
no provision left to sustaine them, and sometimes when they have removed,
they have left us so bare for want of provision, that we have endured much
hunger, before we could get anything to relieve our want, and if that were too
little, they laid great taxes upon many of us, and compelled us to pay it, and
on all the chiefest of us they laid Sesses for man and horse, every man worth
20, or above 20 pounds by the year, was to set forth a horse and man compleatly

Northumberland, Cumberland, Westmerland, and a part of Lancashire are much impoverished thereby.

But now we aer in great hope, that this black Northern storm will in some time be blown, and it beginning to clear clear already by, meanes of a great Victory obtained by Lieut. Gen. Cromwell, major Gen Lambert against the forces commanded by Duke Hamilton, the Earl of Calender and others, though they were unwilling to fight, and tooke more pleasure in plundering, and free quarter, then in martiall affairs, as should become Souldiers, yet they wre at last compelled to fight (as you shall here anon) or else for ought I known, they must have starv'd in their quarters, beginning rise and oppose them in what parts soever they came, but of this enough, the manner of the Fight was thus Lieut. Gen. Cromwell, having left 2 Regiments of Horse and Foot to secure and block the castle of Scarborough and Pomfract, (and understanding that the Scots had entred Lancashire, and began to seek fresh quarter, he tooke with him the new raised forces of Northampton-shire, Leicester-shire and York-shire, and so joyned with Maj. Gen. Lambert, and their forces being united, they marched in 2 body towards the Scottish quarters, and sent out parties to route the stragling, plundering Scots, and force them from their Head quarters. The Scottish Stragglers cared little for fighting, but still made way before our forces, and gathered towards their Head quarters.

Our Forces thus chasing them, gave a strong alarum to the whole Scottish Army, who when they saw there was no remedy, began to make preparation for a sudden engagement. Our forces very resolutely marcht towards them, with an intent to fight them, or force them to a retreat.

The Scottish Forces preceiving the gallant resolution and intention of our soldiers, and seeing they were necessitated to a present engagement, seemed very willing and desirous to try one bout before they returned; wherefore they immediately drew all their forces, both foot and horse into Batalia, and made choise of their ground near a Town in Lancashire, called Preston, some 12 miles from the City of Lancaster; where find a commodious piece of ground for their purpose, both Armies prepared for the fight, and drew their Armiesn to two bodies upon Barbers Moor.

The Scots being first deawne up, got the wind and the most advantagious ground; but yet our Forces would not be discouraged, but resolved to fight though with some disadvantage, both Armies faced each other, we being about 12 or 13 thousand, and the Scots above 20 thousand; parties were drawn out on both sides, who met together and fought, in the mean time both Armies prepared themselves for a charge, and our party overcame the Scots parties, this put us in some hopes of victory, we receiving it for a good Omen: then fresh parties were drawnout, and fought again, and at the last the whole bodyes drew up to the charge, both parties at the first engaged couragiously, and after some dispute, our Infantry being the left Wing, was like to have been worsted, and being overpowered by their numbers, were forced to give ground a little, but yet maintained it with great courage.

While this dispute lasted, our right Wing worsted the Scots, and quite defeated their Cavalry, for after the Scottish Horse had stood to it a charge or two, and finding such not service, began to retreat, our horse followed them, and with their shot to galled them, that they forced them to run, our forces persued them as farre as they could, and not be endangered by the Scottish foot. In this persuit many were slain, and divers taken prisoners. Then our horse retreated, and came in very good time to relieve our left Wing, which was in great danger of being defeated; when they came, they found them to have lost some of their ground, but by the comming in of our horse they were much comforted and encouraged, they having endured two hours of very hot service, the Canons playing often on both sides; then our horse began to charge the Scottish Infantry, who began to be greatly disheartened by seeing their Chavalry thus defeated, and a great part of our Chavalry comming in to assist our left Wing, they charged the Scots again and recovered their lost ground; and udon the second charge the Scots retreated, and were put to a confused flight, our forces persued them till the nghr parted them, and had the pillage of the field.

In this fight we took eighteen hundred prisoners, many of them being men of note, in the next I shall give you a List of the particulars. In the persuit we likewise rescued all the prisoners they had taken, at the beginning of the fight, aud flew 700 of them in the place, wounded many, Duke Hamilton himself narrowly escaping. We took 1100 Horse, 47 Colours, 10 peeces of Ordnance, most of their Carriages and Ammunition, and above four thousand Armes. The Scottish horse are fled towards Scotland, but Lieutenant Generall Cromwell hath sent a partee of horse (if it bee possible) to get before them and stop them. With the next I will all give you a more particular Relation, take this for the present, from

Your assured Friend,
J. Walton.

Aug. 20 1648

A copy of Prince Charles his Letter to the Lord General Fairfax.

My Lord,

eing informed that some rigorous cause is intended against M. G. Laughhorn, C. Powell, C. Poyer, and others now prisoners of war, for things done under the authority of my commission, I thinke fit to let you know, that I cannot but be extreamly sensible of such proceedings, as well in regard of the persons, and of my owne honour, which I take to be highly concerned in their preservation, as also because thereby a necessity will bee put upon mee of proceeding with such as shall fall in to my hands in a way very contrary to my nature, and as far from my intentions, unlesse I be necessitated thereunto by your rigour to those Gentlemen, I desire therefore that by your care and seasonable interposition, such modernation may be used toward them, as becomes Souldiers to one another, and as I conceive to be due to them, which will be an ingagement to me to pursue my inclination towards those that shall be in my power, and so I remain.

Your loving Friend,

Aug.14.1648.

His Excellencies answer.

May it please your Highnesse,

 Have acquainted the Houses with your Highnesses Letter concerning M. G. Laughorn and the rest, it being not in my power to act further, the Parliament having ordered in what way they shall be proceeded against, not so much that they were in hostility against them (I suppose) as that they have betrayed the trust reposed in them to the sad ingaging this Nation in a second Warre and bloudy fait is not in my power to interpose their justice; but that all obstacles of a just and firme peace may be removed, that be the earnest prayer of

Your Highnesses most humble servant.

14 Aug. 1648.

FAIRFAX.

FINIS

An Impartiall

RELATION

of

THE LATE FIGHT AT PRESTON
Being the Copy of a Letter, written (as the Tenour of it importeth)
by Sir *Marmaduke Langdale.*

Sir,

his will give you a finall account of my imployment, which is now ended; being a Prisoner in Nottingham Castle, where I have civill usage. You have heard the condition I was in at Settle and Sigleswick, with about 3000 Foot and 600 Horse, the 13. of August, where hearing the Parliament Forces were gathered together, and Marching towards me, I went to acquaint Duke Hamiliton therewith to Horneby, where he determined for Preston, where (his Army being numerous in Foot) he might have the greater advantage upon his Enemy in those inclosed Countries. I Marched neere Clitherow towards Preston, in the March I met with the Lord Callender and divers of the Scottish Officers Quartered in my way, with whom I was resolved to March to Preston, but for the present the Intelligence was, that the Parliament Forces were divided, some part whereof wre marched to Colne, and so to Manchester, to relieve that Towne in case we should presse upon it. This made the Officers of Horse more negligent of repayring to Preston, but Quartered wide in the Country; the same night certaine intelligence came, that Lieutenant Generall Cromwell With all his Forces was within 3. miles of my Quarters, which I imediately sent to the Duke, and told it to my Lord Leviston, to acquaint Lieutenant Generall Middleton therewith, and drew my Froces together in a field, and so marched towards Preston betimes in the morning where I found the Duke and Lord Callender with most part of the Scottish Foot drawne up; their resolution was to march to Wiggan, giving little credit to the Intelligence that came the night before, but suffer their Horse to continue in their Quarters 10. and 12. miles off; Within halfe an hower of our meeting, and by that time I was drawne into the Close neere Preston, the Enemy appear'd with a small body of Horse: The Scots continue their resolution for Wiggan, for which end they drew their Foote over the Bridge. The Enemy comming the same way that I had marched fell upon my Quarter, where we continued skirmishing fix houres, in all which time the Scots sent me no reliefe: they had very few Horse come up, so as those they sent me at last were but few, and were soone beaten; but if they had sent me 1000 Foote to have flanked the Enemy, I doubt not but the day had been ours.

Yet I kept my post with various successe, many times gathering ground of the Enemy, and as the Scots acknowledg they never saw any Foote fight better then mine did: The Duke being incredulous that it was the whole Army sent Sir Lewis Dives to me; to whome I answered that it was impossible any Forces that were inconsiderable would adventure to presse upon so great an Army as we had, therefore he might conclude it was all the power they could make, and with which they were resolved to put all to the hazard, therefore desired that I might be seconded, and have more Powder and Ammunition, I having spent 9. Barrels of Powder: The Scots continue their March over the River, and did not secure a Lane neere the Bridge, whereby the Parliament Forces came upon my flankes; Neither did the Forces that were left for my supply, come to my relief, but continued in the Reare of mine, nor did they ever face the Enemy but in bringing up the Reare; When most part of the Scots were drawne over the Bridge, the Parliment Forces pressed hard upon me in the Van, and Flankes; and so drive me into the Towne, where the Duke was in person, with some few Horse, but all being lost, Retreated over a Foord to his Foote; After my Forces were beaten, the Parliament Forces beat the Scots from the Bridge presently, and so came over into all the Lanes that we could not joyne with the Foote, but were forced to Charlow, where we found Lieutenant Generall Middleton ready to advance towards Preston to the Foote, which he did; but not finding them there, returned to Wiggan, where the Duke was with his Foote, (mine totally lost.) There they tooke a resolution to go to my Lord Biron, for which end they would march that night to Warrington: In their march to Parliament Forces fell so fast upon their Reare, that they could not reach Warrington that night. And Lieutenant Generall Middleton finding himselfe unable to withstand their Forces, left the Foote in Warrington to make their owne conditions: So as we marched towards Malpas, fix of the Scottish Lords in this march left us, whereof my Lord Traquaire was one; Most part submitted to the Sheriff of Shropshire, who sent two Gentlemen of that County to the Duke to offer him the same Quarter that the Earl of Traquaire had: From Malpas we marched to Drayton, and so to Stone; in our march from thence to Utoxeter the Parliament Forces fell upon the Reare and tooke Lieutenant Generall Middleton; At Utoxeter the next morning going to attend the Duke for his resolution, I found him extreame sick, not able to March; My Lord Callender seemed to refuse all wayes of Treaty, but rather to march Northward where we had a considerable Force, and the whole Kingdome of Scotland at our backs, upon this we marched over the River toward Ashburne; I had the Van, and was marching, presently my Lord of Callender came to me, told me he would march with me, but that none of his Forces would, and that he had much ado to escape them; that he was come himself alone, his Horse pricked in the foote, and without a cloake. I perswaded his Lordship that it was better to returne to his Forces, because I could not protect him, and seeing the Scots had left me, I was resolved to fever, and shift every man for himself; but to capitulate I could not with a safe conscience: After some little discourse he returned to his Forces, and I marched towards Nottingham, where those few I had, tooke feverall wayes, and I got that night over Trent, and came to a house 6. miles from Nottingham, where My selfe, Collonel Owen, Lieutenant Collonel Galliard, and Major Constable, thought to have shrowded our selves as Parliamenteeres, and so made no resistance, but were discovered, and are now in Nottingham Castle this 26 of August 1648.

FINIS.

A Copy of Lieutanant Generall Crumwell's Letter

Gentlemen,

t hath pleased God, this day, to shew a geat mercy to this poore kingdome, by making the Army successefull against the common Enemy. We lay the last night at Mr. Sherburns, of Stamerhurst, about 9 miles from Preston, which was within three miles of the Scots quarters, we advanced this morning betime towards Preston, with a desire to engage the Enemy, and by that time our forlorn had engaged the enemy, we were about foure miles from Preston, and thereupon wee advanced with the whole Army; and the Enemy being drawn out upon a Moore betwixt us & the Town, the Armies on both sides ingaged, and after a very sharpe dispute, continuing for three or four houres, it pleased God to inable us to give the Enemy a defeat, which I hope we shall improve by Gods assistance, to their utter ruine, and in this service your Countrymen have not the least share, which wee cannot expresse by particular, having not time to take an accounts of the slain, and the prisoners, and many of those of quality, and many slain, and the Army disipated. A principall part whereof (with Duke Hambleton) is on the South side of the Ribb, and Darwentbridge, and wee lying with the greatest part of the Army close to them nothing hindring engageing of that part of the Enemies Army but the night; It will be our care that they shall not passe over any Ford beneath the Bridge, to goe Northward, nor to come over betwixt us and Whaley we understand that three Companies of Col. General Ashton are at Whalley, we have 7 Troops of Horse and Dragoons, that we beleeve all at or neer Clithero. This night I have sent order expresly to them to march to Whalley, to joyne with those Companies that you shall improve of your Country Forces, toward the ruine of those enemies: you perceive by this how things stand, by this means the enemy is broken, most of the Horse being gone Northward, and wee having sent a considerable party at the very heeles of them, and the Enemy having lost almost all their Ammunition, and neer 4000 Armes, so that the greatest part of the Foot are naked: Therefore in order to this work we desire you to raise your County, and to improve those forces for the totall ruine of the enemy, which way soever they goe. And if you shall accordingly doe you part, doubt not of their totall ruine. Wee thought fit to speed this unto you to the end you may not bee troubled if they shall march towards you, but improve your interest aforesaid. And that you may give glory to God for this unspeakable mercy from

Your humble Servant
Preston 17 August 1648.
OLIVER CRUMWELL

Noble Sir,

 ieutenant Generall Crumwell sent a Letter to the Committee here, a copy whereof you will receive inclosed; we had also other Letters from other Officers, which gives us advertisements of a glorious victory obtained against the Scots, and English Cavaliers.

Lieutenant Generall Crumwell having falne down with his Army (after conjunction with Collonell Gen. Lambert) out of Yorkeshire, by Clithero, towards the Scots: upon Thursday last engaged with them neer to Preston. Hee hath given them a very great rout, taken 4000 Armes, most of their Ammunition, many prisoners, whereof divers of quality, and is still in pursuite, adding every houre to the number of the slain, and prisoners, and of divers of the Scots that are dispiersed in 6, 8, or 10 in a company, the Country people rise and knock them in the head, where they meet with them; and Lieutenant Generall Crumwells horse are at the very heeles of the Scots horse, that are fled Northwards; the rest of their horse, and body of foot (which escaped by reason of the night) being ill armed, quartered with Duke Hambleton, between Wygon and Preston, being about 8 or 9000. The Lieutenant Generalls Army went towards Preston to waite on them, I hope they will have their fatall blow, for their perfideousnesse, to be an example to Generations to come hereafter. We have had the Country hereabouts in Armes this week, and hope to prevent the Scots passage this way. Cheshire also, I doubt not but will be in readinesse to stop them about Warrington. Another party is about whaley, in Blackburn Hundred.

Sir, I beseech you, if any shew themselves so little lovers of England, as to speak or move for a cessation to oppose it: Let us not adde the further guilt of blood of friends, upon our selves.

Yesterday being Friday, Lieutenant Genrall Crumwell having kild and taken diverse of the Scots, dispersed their body severall ways, The greatest part of them fled towards Warrington, and our Forces still pursuing them; divers of the Country Froces being joyned to assist Lieutenant Generall Crumwell. Some of the Scots were last night at Lansford on Cheshire side, our Army is at their heels: The greatest execution yesterday was about Standish Moore, where divers wre kild and taken, and amongst them many considerable men, both Scatch and English, Duke Hambleton was last night in Wygan.

This morning they are at them again, fresh prisoners brought in hourely, and Armes in abundance. The poore Country people being over joyed at this great deliverance, wherein the Lord hath been wonderfully seen, in delivering us from this faithlesse insulting cruell people.

Manchester the 19 of August, 1648

A List of the great Victory obtained by Lieutenant Generall Crumwell, in the great defeat given to the Scots Army, on Thursday, Friday, and Saturday, August 17, 18, 19. 1648

2500 slain,

2000 taken prisoners,

300 Officers killd & taken

400 Horse taken,

4000 fire armes taken,

2000 armes more taken,

30 Colours taken,

8 Barrels of powder,

4 cartload of Amunition,

Duke Hamilton fled into Wigan and there beset. Sir Marmaduke Langdale fled towards Carlisle, and pursued by Li. Ge. Crumwels horse.

500 cattle retaken that they had plundered from the Country.

5000l. worth of goods restored, that the Scots were sending into Scotland. Divers papers taken of overtures with Pr. Charles, and with some about London.

15000 kild, taken, dispersed, and fled.

Index